POCKE⸱   ⸱⸱

of

THE HORSE

HAZEL M. PEEL

TABB HOUSE
PADSTOW

Published 2000
by Tabb House, 7 Church Street, Padstow
Cornwall, PL28 8BG

First Edition, *Pocket Dictionary of the Horse*, published 1978
by Abson Books
Copyright © Hazel M. Peel 2000

ISBN 1873951 34 5

Illustrations pp. 18, 97, 111, & 112 are by Michael Bowkett
and pp. 56, 57, 60, 73, 84, 99 & 105 by Susan Cutting.

Permission to publish the cover photograph
by Mrs T. Spargo of Wapley Stables, Wapley, Bristol
is gratefully acknowledged.

Printed by TJ International Ltd, Padstow, Cornwall

───────────

Dedicated to all those who ride for fun -
whether they be seven years or seventy.

A POCKET DICTIONARY OF THE HORSE

ACNE. A contagious infection that can be communicated to man. Because of this the strictest hygiene must be observed. The disease begins with spots on the skin which are hot and painful when touched. These turn into unpleasant discharging pustules. A veterinary practitioner should always be called.

Great care must be taken to ensure that the disease is not carried to other horses via the grooming equipment. All stable litter must be burned, the horse kept in isolation and the groom must not be sparing with the soap and scrubbing brush either.

AGE. A mystery in the female of our sex but an open book with the horse! The easiest way is by examination of the teeth. The front incisor teeth are called the Centrals, those next to them the Laterals and finally come the Corner teeth. The Centrals appear in place of the milk teeth at about two years of age, the Laterals at about three and a half years while the Corner teeth should be seen between four and five years. In the male, the Tush appears at five years. Females do not usually have Tushes though there is always the exception to the rule! At six years, the visible small black spots on the Central teeth start to disappear. At seven the spots on the Laterals disappear and at eight years the Corner teeth have lost their spots as well.

By now, the horse is called 'aged' or 'out of the mark'. At nine years a triangular formation commences on the corner incisors and, as the animal ages, this becomes more pronounced. The teeth lengthen. This is clearly seen when the jaws are shut and the lips eased back because the teeth meet at an angle. On the average, unlike us, a horse's teeth and feet wear out before his arteries.

Some horses live very ripe, old lives up to 35 years and even 40 years but this is exceptional. Usually at 17 years a horse is past vigorous work though many riding animals still enjoy a spin and more than one 20 year old can greet the day-break with an exhibition of bucking to delight a cowboy! See also LONG IN THE TOOTH.

AIDS. These are indications which tell the horse what is expected of him. The trouble is that a lot of riders don't learn them and sometimes the horse can learn them more quickly than a dull-witted, ham-fisted supposedly better-brained human! There are two categories of aids: live and mechanical.

The live aids are given with the leg, hand, wrist and bodily sway. Leg aids must be given by touching the animal's flanks which, at this particular spot, are especially responsive owing to the location of a group of sensory nerves. In a well-bred horse these nerves are acutely developed. On no account should the heels be dug in roughly unless the rider wishes to test the speed at which he can bite the dust!

The leg aids should always be given in conjunction with hands and wrists instructing down the reins. As the legs drive the horse forward so the hands and wrists restrain. The horse is 'collected'.

The hands and wrists control all that part of the horse in front of the saddle while the legs control the rear – the engine part. The rider uses his body weight to help by easing it backwards, forwards or sideways.

To go forward apply equal pressure with both legs and relax the reins. To apply the brakes – quite easy with the well-trained horse – feel on the reigns and drag back gently with the legs. Once the horse has stopped, relax these pressures otherwise the trained horse is just as likely to keep reversing. This action can be disconcerting at times!

A horse should be trained to understand the slightest pressure of the rein when laid against the neck. This is called neck-reining. When the right rein is laid across the neck to the left and pressure applied with the right leg, the horse will turn to the left and vice versa.

A good animal should be capable of turning on his forehand (the front legs) or on his haunches. Polo ponies have to be expert at the latter and polo riders soon acquire good, firm riding seats, or take up fishing instead!

There are two flexions: direct and lateral. In the direct flexion the horse bends his neck at the poll and relaxes his jaw to the bit. In the lateral flexion the animal turns his head to right or left, at the same time bending his neck at the poll and giving back his jaw to the rider.

The orders for these movements are given with the wrists on the reins, the legs behind the girth and a slight sway of the body.

Infinite patience is needed to teach a horse the aids. The rewards are found in the absolute joy of riding a trained horse: the smooth ride, the polished responses and the sheer fun of unison with the animal. Constant repetition is the only tutor and once the horse understands what is wanted of him he should be 'made much of'.

The mechanical aids are created by Martingales, nose-bands, whips and spurs. The spur – if used correctly – is the best of the lot because the horse cannot anticipate its use.

ALBINO. A horse whose skin is pink with white or cream hairs. The eyes are often pink as well. Occasionally the skin may also be white and, rarely, black. A true albino is the rarest of colours. They may sometimes be found in Arabians. In the USA the variety is recognised by a specific club.

ALOE. A plant whose dried juice is a valuable purgative. It is a common base for the old fashioned veterinarian's physic ball but it must only be used under professional supervision. In certain circumstances Aloe juice can be dangerous to old horses and pregnant mares.

ANAEMIA. This is a symptom rather than a disease, according to some vets, though there is a strain caused by the Equine Infectious Anaemia virus. It is serious and you must get the vet just as you would get the GP for yourself. In horses and mules it is contagious.

ANAESTHETICS. Drugs administered against pain. Under the Protection of Animals (Anaesthetics) Act, except in the case of an absolute emergency anaesthetics can only be administered by a registered and fully qualified veterinary practitioner .

ANDALUSIAN. A delightful Spanish breed of horse used extensively for the handling of wild fighting bulls in the open countryside. They have a calm temperament and the ability to make astonishingly rapid turns. They are not as fast as the Thoroughbred but with their grace, strength and beauty are prized as riding animals. Their blood has received numerous infusions of the Arabian and the classic Andalusian head shows the familiar Arabian concave face.

ANGLO-ARAB. A splendid breed of horse derived from crossing a Thoroughbred with an Arabian. This breed stands apart and is next to the Thoroughbred where true speed is concerned.

They make splendid riding animals with the usual cross

being a Thoroughbred sire and Arabian dam. A two-thirds Thoroughbred to one-part Arabian also makes a good riding horse. It is important, though, to choose the right horses for the mating. Not every Thoroughbred or Arabian will do. The points to be avoided like the plague are a weedy Thoroughbred or a coarse Arabian.

A useful point to remember in breeding is that excess weight is better on the dam's side.

The Anglo-Arab is less hot to handle than the pure Arabian; he also has more rein in front of the saddle. He is almost the ideal hunter.

ANTHRAX. A most serious and frightful disease occurring in nearly all animals and transmutable to man. This disease is practically world-wide in location. It is caused by a bacillus and its spores. Fortunately, it is rare in Great Britain but is one of the 'notifiable' diseases. All suspected cases must be reported to the police forthwith, if not sooner!

There are two forms. One in the thorax and neck; the other abdominal. Basic signs are swellings at the throat and neck, fever, immobility, laboured breathing and the inability to swallow. Long before the horse has reached this stage professional assistance will have recognised the enemy.

Such is the virulence of the disease that people in contact with animals suspected of Anthrax are fools if they don't go hot-foot to their doctors.

British law totally forbids the disposal of an anthrax carcass except by those authorised to do this thankless job.

APPALOOSA. A beautiful breed of spotted horse of great antiquity, found more in the USA than in Britain and once greatly prized as war horses by the Nez Perce Indians.

The spots vary in colour, shape and size. Some of the variations are white foundations with oval spots, small

5

spots in front and large behind, a dark front with dark spots and white hips. A white animal with large black spots is known as a leopard; a horse without spots at the rear is called a snowstorm horse.

These animals have a lovely disposition, are full of life and easy to manage. One rarer variety, known as Colorado Rangers, have dark bodies with white spots or white with chestnut spots.

APPLE. The horse, like Eve, is easily tempted by an apple. However, if old apples are given, stomach upsets can arise from fermentation in the belly. Don't let the horse make a pig of himself with apples. He'll feel every bit as bad as the boy who steals green apples from the tree, stuffs himself, then wonders why on earth he did it in the first place!

APPRENTICE ALLOWANCE. This is the British weight allowance which a young jockey may claim to offset his inexperience. A horse who is to be ridden by an apprentice rider may have his weight reduced by seven pounds in a race. If he has five winners to his credit, though, the boy can only claim five pounds. If he has ridden forty winners he has, quite simply, had it. He must go out there and battle alone. A man among the men!

ARAB. The world's most ancient breed of horse. The Arab or Arabian is a different species from all other horses in his basic construction. The ordinary horse has six lumbar vertebrae; the Arabian has five. The Arabian has seventeen pairs of ribs to the ordinary horse's eighteen or nineteen pairs. He also has only sixteen tail vertebrae instead of the usual eighteen.

The head of the Arabian is one of the most elegant horse heads in the world, the dream of artists and sculptors. The eyes are wide and bold with flaring intelligence. Arabians have lashes to make any mere woman swoon with envy, tiny, delicate ears and a small, dainty muzzle which should fit neatly into a pint-pot. Above all, though, is the concave bone structure of the nose, the Arabian's trade mark.

The mouth bars are longer with shorter cheek teeth than in the ordinary horse. The facial bones are delicate, like fine china; the eye sockets enormous; the nostrils capable of fantastic expansion and the whole of this marvellous head placed neatly on a highly-arched neck.

The withers must be higher than the quarters with a tail carried very high with the hairs streaming like a flag in a gale. The skin is fine with a silky gloss.

There is so much beauty, elegance and quality in an Arabian that the writer is inclined to wonder why this gorgeous creature allows itself to associate with mere man.

The most common colours are bay, brown, grey and chestnut. Black and pure white are extremely rare as well as highly prized.

The Arabian is full of life and fire in all paces. He is a bold animal but also generous and affectionate if treated kindly. An Arabian resents being shouted at or bullied.

These animals have a different, more pleasant body odour than ordinary horses while their neigh is both musical and enchanting. Many people do not care to ride an Arabian because of his smaller front and tempestuous fire but he has a magic quality which he gives to an understanding rider. An Arabian makes the rider into a monarch. One of the most fantastic rides I had was on an Arabian stallion over the Egyptian desert. Not one of the hundreds of horses I have ridden – before or since – made me feel quite so important. On that ride I did, indeed, become a queen.

The Arab has been used the world over for improving other breeds because his prepotency is incredible. The fine Arabian quality always comes to the fore.

Where out-and-out speed is concerned the Arab cannot touch the Thoroughbred but for stamina, endurance and long-distance riding he is supreme.

The breed of the Arabian goes back more than 5,000 years and there are many references to these horses in the Bible. Many countries in the world have an Arab Horse Society.

ARM. That part of the horse from the elbow under the chest to the knee joint.

ARMY REVERSIBLE. One of the Pelham variety of bits much favoured by armies and police forces and in the author's opinion, one of the best ever invented. This is a bit which suits most horses, being neither too gentle nor too harsh. With its elbowed curb a horse is unable to grab hold of his bit.

ARTIFICIAL RESPIRATION. We all know what this means but trying it on a horse is no joke.

Respiration can be attempted by quickly removing all restraining tack, girths, etc. and, if in the stable, opening wide the door and windows and, with help, turning the horse so that his head is, if possible, downhill.

The ribs should be compressed and released about every four or five seconds; the easiest way to do this is for someone to sit astride the animal and press and release with the body's weight. It helps if the animal can be turned over. If there is no response and the animal can be turned over, try again on the other side. A strong solution of ammonia on a rag placed within a foot of the nostrils may help.

When the horse is down try to get the head and neck in a straight line with the tongue to one side. If water or vomit is suspected try to get the neck higher than the head.

Any action must be swift. A person caught alone with a large animal is in an unenviable situation.

ARVE. An old-fashioned British word for 'left', the opposite to 'heck' meaning right. It used to be used with cart horses in country districts.

ASS. An ass or donkey is different from a horse in that he has an erect mane, a tufted tail and long ears. Grey is the most common colour. If handled with care and kindness an ass can show intelligence.

AZOTURIA. A disease the cause of which is still unknown but which rarely appears in horses under four years of age. Rich living, lack of exercise and wet stables are conditions which breed it. The symptoms can sometimes be seen after exercise. The hind legs are weak; the animal staggers and colic-like symptoms appear. The urine also changes colour. Always obtain instant professional help but remember prevention is better than cure. Rich, idle living won't do you any good either! Hard work never harmed man or beast yet and the plain, simple diet is better for all concerned.

BACKING. A term used to denote the occasion when a young horse first receives a rider on his back. Before this, he should have been accustomed to the feel of the saddle itself. A wise rider backs his horse after the animal has been lunged. It is usual to lie across the saddle the first day before actually getting astride.

It is vitally important the rider is not thrown because it can frighten the horse, to say nothing of giving him the most enormous superiority complex!

9

Caution and patience are required. Assistants should steady the animal as well as distract his attention while the rider swings, gently, into the saddle.

Some horses take great fright when, out of their eye corner, they first see the rider's off-side leg. Be prepared! Put a stirrup leather around the colt's neck so that if he does plunge about you can hold that and not jog his tender mouth. Keep the first lesson short. The colt's back muscles will soon tire. Never hurry. Be patient. Remember, man is supposed to have the superior brains and intelligence! Display yours by understanding the colt's worries and fears. Make much of him.

BACK-UP. That very peculiar action of the fresh horse when he arches his back and warns his rider that it's a grand, frosty morning and he just feels like letting all hell break loose! You have been warned – so sit tight!

BADMINTON. See THREE DAY EVENTS.

BALANCE. Every bit as important as grip! Where sheer brute strength is concerned a mere human is a babe compared to a powerful horse.

BALANCE GIRTH. A strap used on a lady's side-saddle. It is fastened on the right side and offsets the lady's legs on the left. It is crucial that the girth be tight. A lady's life depends on this girth when jumping out hunting.

BALLING. To force a medicine ball down a horse's throat – usually against his will! Medicine is mixed into a ball about two inches long and half an inch wide with a sticky substance like treacle or honey.

An assistant steadies the animal. The ball is held in the first three fingers of the right hand. The horse's tongue is held between its teeth on the opposite side making the animal open his jaws. The medicine ball is popped into the mouth, as far back as possible, the tongue is released, the head pushed up and, hey presto! down goes the medicine – usually!

Some cunning old horses will hold the ball while others spit nearly as well as camels. Push their heads as high a possible, keep them there, and wait until someone gets tired first. It's usually you – but don't let the horse know that! With a really contrary animal a veterinary may have to use a balling gun and 'shoot' the ball down the throat but skill is needed for this.

As a swallowed ball goes down the throat it should be clearly visible on the left side of the neck as a moving swelling.

BALLOTADE. An Haute École term describing a controlled jump performed by the horse. The legs are gathered under the animal's body with the hind hooves turning outwards.

BANDAGES. There are two kinds of bandages: those used to protect wounds and as a medical support; others for legs and tails.

A tail bandage is made of a thick cotton or stockinette material and is complete with tapes. Put the bandage on from the top of the tail working downwards to the end of the tail bones. Tie the tapes in a dapper bow. This is used as a protection for those ridiculous horses who insist upon rubbing their tails and spoiling their otherwise sartorial dress!

Leg bandages are used both in and out of the stable. For stable use they are taken below the fetlock joint. At exercise, though, they should never go round the joint but only support the tendons. For exercise or work they should be wound over cotton wool and stitched into place.

When not in use keep bandages rolled neatly with the

tapes inside. Bandaging for medical purposes can prove a problem because of a horse's size and the fantastic dexterity of his teeth! Shoulder and breast bandages can be fixed to the roller. Loin and quarter bandages can also be fixed this way but it is wise, for the sake of the rider's blood pressure, to get the professional's help. It is sometimes necessary to put a cradle on the horse to stop him tearing his bandages into minute sections the moment your back is turned.

BANG-TAIL. An expression used to describe a tail cut off straight with scissors. Can also be used, though, to describe a horse whose tail has been left as nature intended, i.e. undocked, unpulled.

BARB. The name Barb originally came from the horses found on the North and North-West African coast. They were a cold-blooded type of animal with large heads, thick necks and coarse faces.

At one stage in history the term Barb referred to any horse from foreign or barbaric parts.

BAREBACK. To ride without a saddle. The rider needs a strong grip, pure balance and a non-slip bottom! The easiest gait is the canter; the most bone-shattering a trot. A horse with too high withers is most uncomfortable while one whose withers are too low becomes too slippery. All riders should, at some stage, try their skill at riding bareback.

BARLEY. Barley is a grain which is better boiled and fed to the horse when the grains can be squashed between the fingers. Raw, natural barley is a very heating, rich food. Some people, though, do feed crushed barley and it has been found good for hard-working ponies as it doesn't go to their heads too much!

If a newly-born foal has a very loose bowel action the matter can often be remedied by giving the dam a handful of dry barley. This clears up the dam's milk and stops the foal's looseness or scouring.

BARS OF THE FOOT. That part of the foot where the wall turns inwards and forwards. Bars are a strong part of the foot and are an important resting surface for the shoe.

BARS OF THE MOUTH. These are the natural positions in the mouth which man has cleverly utilised for the position of the bit. They are most sensitive and a heavy-handed rider can inflict great pain with a sharp bit.

BATHS. In Britain the climate is not exactly suitable for bathing horses, unlike kindlier climes! If though, through a parasitic infection, bathing becomes necessary care must be taken to ensure the horse is dried properly – and I do mean properly!

It is usual to empty buckets of soft, hot, soapy water over the horse and work into the coat with the hands or soft brush. Do rinse the soap out thoroughly, remove the excess water with a body scraper then get busy with towels and clean straw. Pay great attention to drying the genitals, the belly, the loins, heels and the ears.

You will be exhausted by the time you have finished. But the horse should feel fine and he is more important than you!

It is wise to put some clean fresh straw under a blanket and leave the horse with a nice, warm mash. Do not, of course, bath the horse when the east wind is blowing.

BATTLE HORSE. The early British animals were mere ponies and quite unsuited for carrying knights in their heavy armour. As early as 1200 King John imported 100 dray stallions into Britain to put some bone and strength into the native animals. As knights and armour became heavier so the horses were bred bigger and stronger but in the process lost speed. The huge King Henry VIII became alarmed at the lack of heavy battle horses and passed laws that compelled men to breed for weight and strength alone. It is to these heavy horses that the splendid English Shires owe their descent.

Oliver Cromwell sounded their death knell. He had the wit to see that battles could be won with fewer men, moving more easily on faster, light-weight horses. He is the father of the light cavalry (*q.v.*).

BAY. A lovely colour ranging from bright bay to dark brown. This colour is easily distinguished from the similar chestnut because a bay always has a black mane and tail and usually black legs below the knee.

BEANS. Beans are another heating food like barley and should be given sparingly and well-cooked. Feed in a mash form.

BEDDING. A horse's bed may be composed of many materials, some old fashioned like straw, others far more modern and not always better for it either.

Before the advent of the combine harvester, **wheat**, when cut, was stacked to dry and the straw that came to stables was composed of long fronds which made perfect beds. Now it is baled and will arrive bent, broken and twisted. Because of this, it fails to act as it should because of the squashed fronds.

Some owners go for **sawdust** which is fine provided it is minus nails, splinters and other undesirable objects. Sawdust clogs in the hooves, unlike old fashioned wheat straw, so they must be cleaned daily.

Shavings are better than sawdust but, again, they

require inspection before the horse is left.

Shredded paper is useful especially for horses which are allergic to dust mites but this bedding does not come at all cheap. It is true horses do not, usually, attempt to eat this type of bedding but unless attended to really regularly, it will develop an offensive smell.

Peat was used by some for a long time but the Green Lobby object to this because of the attacks on the Wetlands to obtain peat. On the other hand, it can be recycled for the garden's use more easily than straw which takes time to compost down.

The most modern type of bedding is a **composite rubber** type material which is expensive and needs preparatory work. The box floor must slope for good drainage and the rubber flooring needs lifting every two or three days, for disinfecting. Horses seem to like rubber floors and they certainly obviate capped hocks but the initial outlay cannot be classed as economical.

Some people go for **sand** but what happens when the horses discovers it contains salt? The next thing you will have is a vet's bill because the animal has been eating the sand to obtain the salt, even if a proper salt lick has been provided!

If straw is used, it should be shaken all around the box to a good depth and piled around the walls as well as under the manger. In the old days it was also the custom to make a fancy plait at the door entrance by intertwining the fronds.

Oat straw has never been as good as that from **wheat** and **barley** should be avoided like the plague because of the sharp tines. Also horses will happily tuck into barley or oat straw even if well fed!

Whatever the type of bedding for which you opt, always remember there is the problem of storage and, with straw, a fire risk if smokers are around. Your insurance might also be higher accordingly.

There are so many pros and cons about bedding today that it is prudent to and visit other stables to see what other people use and, more to the point, how much it all costs.

BISHOPING. A fraudulent and illegal practice of falsifying a horse's age by re-painting in the black spots on the teeth which may have worn away, making the animal appear younger than he is. An experienced eye can detect this ruse because other signs of age are still left, i.e. the angle and length of the teeth.

The name comes from the veterinary who first came across this practice.

BITE. A horse bite is a wound. Treat it as such. See your doctor and obtain an anti-tetanus injection. Do not try and be the local hero.

BITLESS BRIDLES. Bitless bridles are most valuable when a horse's mouth has been damaged or his mouth ruined, which can make him a puller.

These bridles work upon the nostrils with a constricting strap that cuts off the animal's breathing. The most common is called the Hackamore. These bridles were very popular with certain of the American Indian tribes.

BITS. Bits are the objects placed in the horse's mouth to enable the rider to have control. They are made of many substances, the commonest being metal, rubber or vulcanite. They are divided into 3 categories:

> 1. The *snaffle* group
> 2. The *curb* group
> 3. *Combination* bits.

Snaffle bits have the rings outside the mouth and the actual bar may be straight or twisted, in one piece or split into two and held together with a simple joint.

The plain, unbroken, rubber snaffle is the most gentle bit. The side rings, to which are attached the reins, may be in a circle, a D or thickened at one side and called 'egg-butt'. These latter two can never pinch the corners of the mouth.

A vicious type of snaffle is the Gag where tremendous leverage is obtained by running part of the head piece and rein itself through the bit. Only to be used by very experienced riders.

Snaffles are nearly always used on racehorses though they are a popular universal bit. Their invention is lost in history. A snaffle bit lifts the horse's head.

The curb bit works on the lower jaw and is held in place with a chain or restraining strap. The mouthpiece may be unbroken or split into two. It may also have a port which rests on the tongue. The reins fasten onto the curb pieces; the longer the curb the more severe the bit. When the rein moves the bit works on leverage gripping the jaw in a vice.

A curb lowers the head and makes a horse give back his jaw. The opposite to a snaffle.

The combination bits can be divided into two sections:

1. The most popular is the Pelham, which is merely a variety of curb bit with double reins. There are many variations, one of the best being the Army Reversible.

2. The double bridle is, as its name implies, two bits: a curb and a small snaffle called a bridoon. Not all horses

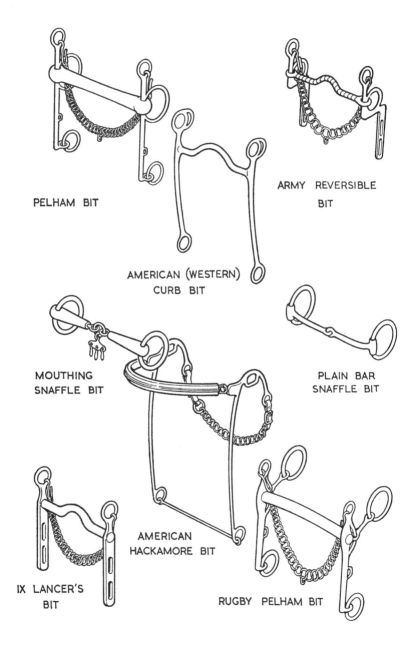

PELHAM BIT

ARMY REVERSIBLE
BIT

AMERICAN (WESTERN)
CURB BIT

MOUTHING
SNAFFLE BIT

PLAIN BAR
SNAFFLE BIT

AMERICAN
HACKAMORE BIT

IX LANCER'S
BIT

RUGBY PELHAM BIT

take kindly to wearing two bits though there is easy control with the bridoon lifting or the curb lowering the head.

The American cowboy always rides with a long curb bit on a very slack rein. The Australian stockman prefers the snaffle bit and a short rein.

The sensible thing is to find the bit which suits the horse. Do not follow the dictates of fashion!

BLACK. A colour which ranges from jet black all over to dark brown with a black muzzle. A pure black is a rare animal. There is an old horsey saying that a pure black is either very, very good or hopelessly bad. There is no in-between.

BLACKSMITH. Many new horsey people say they are going to get the blacksmith to shoe their new horses, which is hopelessly wrong. A blacksmith does not shoe horses because he is a craftsman who works in iron. They mean farrier (*q.v.*).

In an absolute emergency, say, with a loose shoe or one torn off because of thick mud, a blacksmith could engage in a running repair to enable horse and rider to get home, but that is it. His living is not, strictly speaking, shoeing horses.

BLANKET. Usually made of thick wool. The horse wears one next to his body under a canvas rug. The portion of the blanket at the neck should be folded over and tucked under the rug so that it is held firmly in place. See under CLOTHING.

BLAZE. A white stripe down a horse's face which is used as an identification mark.

BLINKERS. Leather blinkers are mostly used on driving

animals to prevent them seeing the moving wheels. They can also be used on riding horses, like race horses, to make them concentrate on what they are doing and gallop straighter.

BLOOD. This is such a vast enormously complicated subject I refuse to write much about it. Only the professional is competent to deal with blood and its associated problems.

How much blood is there in a horse? Very hard to answer. A rough rule of thumb is that the amount of blood in any horse is about 6.6% or 1/15th of the body's weight.

If your horse's blood does not act like our blood then do something about it by calling your vet. You would not hesitate or shilly-shally for yourself so be as quick for your horse.

BLOOD HORSE. This is the colloquial name for a Thoroughbred horse. To say a horse looks as if he has blood, is to pay him a compliment. You are implying he is well bred!

BODY LANGUAGE. All mammals have developed this to a fine art. The writer cannot speak about cold blooded reptiles!

Learn to read a horse's body language because he is certainly learning yours! He can tell from the tone of your voice, your gait and stance, the way and speed with which you move, whether he is doing right or wrong. So obviously he presumes you are bright enough to know his body language!

When he is annoyed back will go his ears. How *far* back will depend upon the depth of his irritation. An uplifted head means alarm and nervousness. The lowered head and poking nose means curiosity. Even the way the legs and feet move are body signs and the tail is an encyclopaedia of information!

If he opens his mouth, curls up his top lip and shows his teeth he is not laughing as the uninitiated think. He is scent testing. Cats also do this with the Jacobson's Organ in the roof of their mouth. We humble humans lack this.

Body language can be read in a horse's gait. Short, mincing steps mean 'Watch out! I'm full of beans and going to play up!' The humped back means the same, giving a warning of a kick or buck to come in the immediate future! His gait can also tell you whether there is a big dragon ahead which means he will whip around in a shy and bolt. If you lose control and become a terrified passenger, the fault is yours for not reading your horse's body language and being prepared.

BOLTING. A frightening equine vice. If a horse bolts the rider can only try to control him by dropping one rein and turning in a circle. A horse can bolt from fright, ill-health or sheer bad temper. If the bolting is caused by temper, change the bit. If an otherwise quiet animal bolts conduct a good investigation into the horse's health. Many horses will bolt in protest if the bit hurts their mouth or if their teeth are bad.

BONES. It is useful to understand the horse's bone structure in relation to that of man. The horse's hock equals the man's ankle.

Bone is also spoken of when describing the width of the cannon bone, i.e. so many inches of bone denoting strength. Clean bone means a leg free from blemishes, especially free from splints.

BOOT. An article of clothing worn on the legs to protect the horse from cutting himself. Some animals have such a swinging stride that the hind hooves cut the forelegs. Boots mitigate this. They can also be worn to stop jumpers hurting their legs going through, instead of over, fences. There are a number of varieties: brushing boots, hock boots, speedy-cutting boots.

BORING. A nasty habit when the horse hangs his head low with all the weight on the rider's arm as he tries to pull him out of the saddle. Correct this by changing to a snaffle bit to keep the head raised. A horse who bores and then bolts is a menace to himself and everyone else around.

BORTHWICK. A type of bit with a mouthpiece extending well away from the lips to minimise sores.

BRAN. This is nothing but the refuse of the grain after milling. It can be fed to horses in a hot mash mixed with other foods. It should be a pale brown colour and not in minute sawdust size particles.

It can act as a mild laxative and will also often tickle the appetite of a tired horse when mixed with hot water, oats, nuts, some sliced apples or carrots.

Some horses have the habit of bolting their bran mash so it is unwise to add too much hard protein to the mix; otherwise this goes straight through the animal unchewed.

BREAKING OUT. Breaking into a sweat. Even if brought back to the stable dry, some horses, through temperament, will promptly break out into a lather of sweat. It is essential to dry them off properly before leaving them for the night and it is a waste of time drying the body unless the ears are dried first.

It helps if the horse is watered, fed, then left to stand quietly with plenty of clean dry straw under his blanket. The air will circulate freely while keeping the animal warm.

BREAST. That part of the horse at the frontal base of the

22

neck and between the forelegs.

BREAST STRAP. These are straps worn around the breast and attached to the saddle to stop it slipping backwards.

BRED HORSE. A well-bred horse, a Thoroughbred.

BREEDING. Puberty in the mare takes place at about sixteen months while the male reaches this a little earlier. The mare will come into season from about February until July. This will last about a week and occur about every three to four weeks.

The best time for service by the stallion is about the ninth day of oestrous or season. The gestation period or pregnancy in the mare is eleven months but a year with the ass.

BREEDS. The various breeds of British horses are as follows:

Heavy	Shire, Clydesdale, Suffolk.
Light-Heavy	Cleveland Bay, Yorkshire Coach Horse, Hackney.
Saddle	Thoroughbred, Arabian, Hunter, Anglo-Arab.
Ponies	Polo, Dartmoor, Exmoor, New Forest, Welsh, Highland, Connemara, Fell and Dale, Shetland, Icelandic.

All of which are discussed under their headings.

BRIDLE. That which the horse wears upon his head. It connects with straps to the bit and reins and consists of a headpiece, throatlash, noseband, side pieces and brow band. This should all be kept clean and supple with saddle soap. See DOUBLE BRIDLE.

BROKEN KNEES. Scars which are carried on the knees from a fall. A horse so marked is suspect and will never fetch a good price.

BROKEN WIND. A weakness of the horse's respiration. Broken wind can follow an illness or it can arise from brutal riding. A persistent cough is an early sign as well as shortness of breath. At fast work a definite roaring can be heard.

There are two operations which the veterinarian can perform for broken wind in its early stages. These are tubing and hobdaying. In a bad case nothing can be done. The animal is useless for riding though, if a mare, there is always the possibility of breeding from her.

A very rough guide for broken wind, when buying a horse without riding him, is to pretend to hit him in the ribs with a stick. If he makes a peculiar grunt - leave him alone and look elsewhere.

BRONCO or Mustang. An American term for a wild range animal.

BROWN. A horse's colour descriptive of its name which may be light oak or dark and almost black.

BRUISES or Contusions. These should be treated with common sense just like human bruises. However, if the bruising is severe call in the vet in case there is muscular damage as well. A bruise around a joint or in the hoof requires professional treatment so it is either the vet or the farrier, or even both.

BRUMBY. An Australian wild horse which roams the out-back often in vast herds. Each herd is led by its own fighting stallion.

BRUSHING. The action when one hoof brushes against the other leg causing bruising and cuts. Boots should be worn as a protection. The farrier can also fit a different type of shoe. Horses who brush themselves regularly have bad action in their gait.

BUCK. A bad habit when a horse leaves the ground and thinks he is heading for the moon. He humps his back, flails his tail, takes off with all four legs and, in short, plays hell. The rider must sit straight and firm. Bucking should be discouraged. Keep the horse's head up. To buck, the animal must get his head down.

BUCKETS. The best modern buckets are those made of rubber or strong plastic, though the old-fashioned, heavy wooden bucket, if kept clean, was good.

Always stand a bucket with the handle away from the horse's head when he drinks. If he happened to get his head under the handle, horse and bucket could well end up on the floor in different directions!

BUCKJUMP RIDER. Men and women who specialise in riding the rough buck-jumping rodeo horses in America and Australia. The prize money is good, the injury risk high. Broken bones are common but the sport is very popular and the high skill required to stay in the saddle much appreciated by audiences.

BUMPING. A term used to denote the pushing and bumping when jockeys ride too close together and their mounts actually hit while racing.

Bumping is also a common name for 'posting' at the trot (*q.v.*).

BURSITIS. Inflammation of a joint, often caused by a fall, an accident or after being kicked. The region is hot and swollen. Don't mess about with it yourself; call in your vet.

BUTCHER. A contemptuous name for a heavy-handed rider who cuts his horse's mouth.

CALKINS. The portion of the horseshoe which turns down at the heel enabling a grip to be obtained.

CANKER A serious foot condition found in wet and filthy stables. The hindfeet seem to be more affected than the fore hooves. There is a nasty, offensive smell. The hooves become soft with the skin above turning red. Get the veterinarian at once. Better still, don't let the condition arise. Look after your horse properly.

CANNON BONE. The long, large bone beneath the horse's knee. It should have good breadth and be free from all blemishes especially splints (*q.v.*).

CANTER. A comfortable, rocking gait.

CANTLE. The rear uppermost part of the saddle.

CAPPED ELBOW. A swelling at the horse's elbow caused by lying on insufficient bedding. It should be softened and treated with hot fermentations. Put more bedding down. Don't let the condition arise! Prevention is much better – and a lot cheaper – than cure!

CAPPED HOCK. The same as for Capped Elbow but applicable to the hock instead.

CAPPED KNEE. And again the same! So much easier to make a thick bed for the horse than cause suffering and a depleted bank balance!

CAPRIOLE. An Haute École movement. A difficult but controlled jump where the horse leaps upwards, stretching its hindlegs to the rear.

CAREERS. See EMPLOYMENT & QUALIFICATIONS.

CARROTS. A vegetable that horses adore. Feed either chopped or in long lengths.

CARTING. A horse who works in harness, pulling a cart.

CAST IN A BOX. A predicament into which horses sometimes put themselves. In other words they are down on the ground in their stable and can't get up. Be quiet. Do not panic. The horse will do enough for both of you! Try to pull the horse away from any obstacle but get help first unless you want a rupture. If there is plenty of bedding kept on the floor and under obstacles like mangers, a horse should not get himself into this position.

A horse is also sometimes 'cast' (thrown) deliberately on the ground for operations. This requires great professional skill to avoid injury. Do not try this yourself.

CAST OFF. A poor type of creature that has been discarded.

CASTRATION. This is only performed on the male animal and, by law, must only be done by a veterinarian under an anaesthetic. The objects are to make the animal more amenable to the will of man and to halt indiscriminate breeding.

CAVALLETTI. Poles or logs laid on the ground and over which, at a trot, the horse is exercised. This teaches him to pick up his feet and keep himself collected. It also makes his back supple.

CAVALRY. Mounted soldiers. When man first mounted a horse and rode him into battle will never be known. It was certainly well before Christ. In the second Book of Kings, horses are described as carrying soldiers into battle.

The great general Genghis Khan ran his hordes of soldiers over Asia. They were mounted on tough little ponies on which they ravaged that continent.

In the Middle Ages knights were so heavily armoured that they had to have a very strong and heavy horse. They were also very slow. The Saracens ran rings around the Crusaders on their swift Arabians with little armour but, of course, they could do no damage to the metal-clad knight. On the other hand he could not catch his enemy.

Stalemate!

Many historians consider that Oliver Cromwell was the first man to use cavalry correctly. He designed leather armour and he selected light, fast animals. This, combined with his superior military tactics, enabled him to win the British Civil War.

He founded the modern cavalry. The Light Brigades were on fast horses and the men carried a sword and lance. The Heavy Brigades were slower with stronger weapons. Everyone has heard of the famous Light Brigade Charge at Balaclava in 1854.

Frederick II of Prussia copied Cromwell's tactics. So did Napoleon; by using Cromwell's selective basis he acquired cavalry to the number of 100,000.

Cavalry lost its purpose during World War I when trenches and static warfare came into being. In World War II cavalry was used only briefly in Poland and Russia.

In this Nuclear Age the cavalry are well and truly obsolete though for ceremonial purposes they make a sight to gladden the eye.

CHAFF. Also called chop. This is made from good quality hay, fed into a machine and cut or chopped into small sections. It is mixed with the horse's feed. It provides good, nourishing bulk.

CHAFING. Chafing of the skin occurs when harness and tack fit incorrectly; the leather is too stiff or the animal has not been properly conditioned. The pain is the same as we suffer with blistered heels. The treatment is likewise. Bathe gently, dust with an antiseptic powder and leave alone until healed then harden the skin gradually with gentle use for short periods.

CHALK JOCKEY. One whose name is unknown and

whose name is chalked up on the number board at race meetings instead of being painted on.

CHANGING LEGS. A horse should always canter on the correct leg and be schooled to change from one leg to the other. The aids must be used correctly. To change from one leading leg to the other the rider feels behind the girth with his leg, alters the position of his body slightly and, at the same time, feels the reins against the horse's neck. The schooled horse responds instantly.

The best way to practice changing legs is by riding a figure-of-eight. It is also wonderful, stomach-stretching, muscle-pulling exercise for the rider!

CHARLIER SHOEING. A special way to shoe. The shoe lacks a toe clip, having instead a groove cut in the hoof itself, and the shoe is sunk to the level of the sole. The object is to protect the foot of an animal out at grass by allowing him to have his most natural footing on all surfaces.

This type of shoeing is highly specialised. If an error is made damage is caused to the sensitive area of the foot.

CHESNUT. A red colour. Known as chesnut in all horses except the Suffolk Punch.

CHESTNUT. This colour ranges from bright red to pale gold. The mane and tail are never black though sometimes they are white or silver.

CHILLS & **COLDS**. They have exactly the same effect as on us and arise from the same causes. The treatment is much the same. Isolation, warmth, light diet, good bedding, sound clothing and rest. The cold will soon run its normal course but if it continues for more than a few days get professional help.

CIRCUS HORSE. Horses are great circus favourites, the

most popular breeds being the Arabian and Hanoverian.

Horses used for vaulting must have a good broad back, very steady pace and unflappable temperament. Those animals used to show Haute École movements are usually the lighter, more nimble Arabs.

CLASS HORSE. A well-bred animal.

CLASSIC RACE. The British Classic Races are:

> The Two Thousand Guineas
> The One Thousand Guineas – for fillies only
> The Derby
> The Oaks – for fillies only
> The St Ledger

No horse has ever won all five although some have won what is known as the Triple Crown, i.e. The Two Thousand Guineas, The Derby and the St Ledger.

CLEAN BRED. A Thoroughbred or animal whose breeding is pure and uncrossed.

CLENCHING. Sometimes called clinching. These are the shoe nails which are seen on the outside of the hoof and which the farrier turns down and rasps off smooth. Sometimes, over the weeks, these nails loosen and they have to be clenched down again.

CLEVELAND BAY. A very old British breed whose colour, as the name suggests, is always Bay. They are large animals reaching between 16 and 16.3 hands. They were originally bred in Yorkshire as coach horses. They are proud-looking, strong, have a good action and, when crossed with a Thoroughbred, make fine hunters.

Sometimes these horses have small stripes on their forearms. This is supposed to show a pure bred, though others argue against the stripes. The only white colouring allowed for showing is on the head in the shape of a star and perhaps just a sprinkling of white hair at the heels.

CLEVER. An animal who knows all about it, whether it be hunting or racing. He often seems to know more than his rider!

CLINCHING. See CLENCHING.

CLIPPING. The object is to remove the thick winter coat and facilitate drying the animal after hard, fast work. An unclipped horse in his winter coat is subject to tiring and unnecessary sweating; it is also difficult to dry him properly in the stable.

There are three ways to clip. The most popular method is to clip the body but leave the coat on the legs as a protection against thorns when jumping. A saddle mark is also left to avoid sores.

The second method is to clip all over. The horse is very easy to clean but, if a jumper, he should wear leg bandages.

The third way is to clip trace high, i.e. as high as the traces of a cart.

Before being clipped the horse should be thoroughly groomed so that the machine blades do not clog. After clipping he should be groomed again. While clipping do not allow the animal to get cold. Cover him with a rug especially over his loins.

Well bred horses' coats grow more slowly than those of half breeds and consequently they need clipping less. After Christmas the coat stops growing altogether until the new Spring coat appears.

One of the usual conditions of a sale is that a horse 'is quiet to clip'.

31

CLIPS. Toe clips are the pieces of the horse shoe which turn upwards and grip the hoof to stop the shoe slipping with use. Front feet have one clip; hind feet two which are placed at the sides of the hoof to stop the horse cutting his front legs when in movement.

CLOTHING. Horses must always wear clothing when clipped. This comprises a thick, woollen blanket under a canvas rug held in place by a roller. If the weather is very cold two blankets can be given.

In good stables rugs are of two kinds. A plain canvas rug for night and a smart gaily coloured rug for day wear.

If the clothing slips at any time it is no good at all just trying to pull it straight. You must take it all off and start again! The correct way is to throw the clothing high on the horse's neck then put it into the correct position by moving with the lie of the hair. With young horses it is wise to be cautious when first putting on the clothing. Quite naturally, many object most strenuously!

When taken out for slow exercise the horse may wear the rug under the saddle with the front part folded into a pleat under the saddle flaps. For fast work, this must be removed altogether.

CLYDESDALE. These animals are considered to be of Scottish origin. This is a very popular working horse with great pulling powers whose colours range from bay, brown and black with the odd chestnut or roan appearing.

They are active animals with plenty of clean bone and large amounts of fine, silky feather at their heels. They grow up to seventeen hands. It is common for them to have a large, white blaze on their heads.

COB. This is a type of horse and not a breed. They are short, thick-set animals standing not more than fifteen hands. They used to have docked tails when that barbaric practice existed. They usually have their manes hogged.

A cob should be tough, quiet and comfortable, capable of carrying a big man many miles without distress and even-tempered enough to be used by the family's children. A good cob can be obtained from an Arabian-Percheron cross.

COLD BACK. This is a well-known condition peculiar to many well-bred horses. They do not like the saddle put on their backs first thing unless it has been warmed. If not, they are liable to object in the most violent manner with a rodeo exhibition of bucking.

Warm your saddle first or alternatively, leave the horse with the saddle on his back in the stable for ten minutes before you mount.

COLD BLOODED. Not well bred.

COLIC. This is a condition to which horses are very prone. It is, loosely, belly ache but much more serious than that which little boys get when they stuff themselves with too many green apples.

The horse is in pain and shows it. He might hump his back, pour with sweat, stare anxiously at his flanks or even try to bite or kick himself.

One possible cause is that of giving cold water to a very hot horse instead of chilling it, but Colic can be caused otherwise. It is a serious condition which can indicate other grave physical troubles. Get the vet quickly. Do not drag your feet because, after only two or even three hours, the horse's condition can worsen to the extent that he dies. The many possible causes are complex and only the vet can help.

COLLAR. Worn by all animals to pull an object. The traces are attached to the collar. The collar should be neither so big that it rubs nor so small that it pinches. Make sure the edges are smooth and pliable. Always put the collar over the head upside down then turn it the correct way when sliding it down the neck.

COLOURS. These are extensive and range through the whole spectrum, from the purest of blacks to the snowiest of whites. In between there is every shade of brown and grey, and spots, dapples and splotches.

The colours go from albino, with pink eyes, down to black via bay, brown, chestnut and dun. Then there are the roans which may be either red or blue, depending on the multi-coloured hair. Some horses have two colours and are either piebald or skewbald. A piebald is black and white whereas a skewbald is any colour except black, with white in very large, irregular patches or splotches.

The Appaloosa horses have spots which, again, break down into various categories. Grey horses range from almost pure white to dappled with two differently coloured hair.

Dun coloured horses are not all that common in Britain as opposed to other countries in the world, especially Mongolia (see Mongolian Horses).

A foal's colour at birth is not always that which it will wear when adult. Many Lipizzaner horse foals are born black or dark brown and do not gain their true colour until five years of age.

People often disagree on a horse's exact colour so the usual rule of thumb is to decide the colour by that shown around the muzzle, excluding stripes of white, of course.

COLOURS also refers to the shirts and caps worn by jockeys in combinations of colours chosen and registered by owners to identify their riders.

COLT. A young male horse is referred to as a colt until he has either been gelded or reached the age of four full years when he becomes an Entire. Once he has been used for breeding he is called a stallion.

COMMON BRED. A horse without quality or pedigree, often having much feather around the leg joints.

CONCAVE SHOE. A specially made horse shoe which is necessary for those animals who over-reach themselves. One edge of the shoe is bevelled: the inside edge.

CONFIDENTIAL. A horse who is 100 per cent quiet in all respects and suitable for the young, the elderly or the nervous to ride.

CONFORMATION. The general make and shape of a horse. Riding animals should always have good sloping shoulders, with short and strong backs and a good length from stifle to hock.

The legs should be clean from all blemishes, the hocks strong, the pasterns neither too long nor too short. The feet should be strong, the quarters round and well muscled with the tail set on square. Only constant observation can teach you what to look for. The best tutor is a stud groom of the old school.

Some definite errors in conformation are:
Ewe-neck, meaning that the neck beds the 'wrong' way.
Herring-gutted, describing a horse weak in the middle.
Cow-hocked, meaning poor hocks shaped like a cow's.
Goose-rumped, indicating a tail set-on too low.

These are a few bad points.

This is a complex art requiring constant study.

CONTAGIOUS DISEASE. Contagious means pollution by physical contact. In other words the sick affect the healthy.

Certain contagious diseases are notifiable by law to the authorities. They include Anthrax, Glanders, Epizootic Lymphangitis, and Parasitic Mange (*q.v.*).

CONTRACTED TENDONS. After severe sprains the tendons of the leg may start to contract and this can be spotted when it is seen that the horse's shoe is wearing down too quickly. The condition is hard to cure but much can be done with high shoe calkins.

CONTUSIONS. See BRUISES.

COPER. An uncomplimentary name for a horse dealer who is not as honest as is expected!

CORNS. Yes! Horses get them too! They can result from a bruise to the sensitive laminae, by bad shoeing or fast work on hard roads. They are very painful. Often the sole has to be pared away to open up the seat of the corn to remove an abscess. The farrier can also fit a special shoe in less severe cases. A poultice and rest can work wonders also.

CORONET. The area where the hoof joins the leg.

COUGH. Treat as for colds and chills. Cough paste is still used now and a again and if it is to be given the easiest way is to smear the sticky mixture on the animal's bit! A coughing horse should *never* be worked in case his wind is damaged. Many horses cough but as long as they 'blow' afterwards it is considered to be all right. See also LARYNX.

COW HOCKS. Also known as Sickle hocks. These are weak hocks which turn inwards and under. They are a conformation fault.

COW PONY. The name for the American cowboy's horse.

CRAB. To make very rude remarks about a horse and his ability. In other words, to slander him!

CRACKED HEELS. These arise from bad stable management and are almost unforgivable. They are caused by horses standing in wet conditions or not having their heels dried properly after work. They are akin to chapped hands in the human.

CRADLE. A device fixed around a horse's neck to prevent him turning and bending his head to lick at medicine or destroy his dressings.

CRASH HELMET. Worn, by law, by all jockeys.

CREAM. A self-descriptive colour which is rather lovely but hard work to keep clean.

CREST. The point midway between the withers and the poll. The crest is always very well developed on the stallion. It is a male characteristic.

CRIB BITING & WIND SUCKING. This is a vice. It is usually learned by young horses and, as often as not, arises from not enough exercise and downright boredom. The horse, to occupy his time and use up too much unexercised energy, starts biting objects, usually those of wood like the stable door.

In the process of this biting the horse sucks in excess air, the palate is forced open and then comes a great swallow. A huge gulp of air goes down the gullet into the stomach, often with a grunt.

The process does not do the teeth all that much good either; they wear away too rapidly. The throat muscles increase in size and shape and the digestive system of the stomach objects most strongly. There might be indigestion as a result, with fermentation of the stomach's contents, none of which is conducive to good equine health, because the horse becomes less fit and condition is lost.

The cure is difficult and often impossible. A tight throat strap might help but this has to be removed for normal feeding. There are also certain bits that might be recommended to you like those of wood or metal which have perforated holes.

It is much more prudent to make sure the condition does not arise in the first place. Exercise the horse properly. Give him a hay net so packed that it takes him most of the day to unpack and eat it! Make sure he has something interesting to look at over his stable door. Always remember that the horse is a very social animal and he likes company or activity; something, anything to pass the time until the next manger feed.

CRIME. Sadly this has reached the horse world with a vengeance. The first step to combat crime is to have your animals freeze marked. It does not hurt them and the letters and numbers go onto a computerised register. As the marks can never be eradicated, they can prove invaluable should an animal be stolen.

The second step is to join the local Horse Watch. This runs on similar lines to Vehicle Watch for cars and Home Watch for houses. Everyone keeps an eye on strangers and others' animals. If there is no Horse Watch in your area then start one. The local police will be delighted to advise and help.

There is nothing more distressing, even heart breaking, to have any animal stolen whether horse, dog or cat.

Saddlery stealing too is, sad to say, big business now. Do make sure all your expensive saddles, bridles and other horsey equipment are kept under firm lock and key. It is better to keep these indoors, where possible, and under a burglar alarm. Also, it is prudent to mark them with an invisible pen with your post code.

Whatever, do not sit back and do nothing in today's criminal society where people think nothing even of stealing plants from gardens! Horses and everything appertaining to them are worth much money. Protect yours, especially the animals. They cannot help themselves, can they?

CRIOLLO. A tough little horse from the Argentine which has descended from the Arab or Barb. The colouring is usually dun or pale brown although piebald and skewbald are not unknown. The maximum height is fifteen hands.

CROUP. The top point of the horse's rounded quarters.

CROUPADE. An Haute École movement when the trained horse leaps forward with its legs tucked under its body.

CRUPPER. Always used on harness horses. This goes under the tail. It can also be used on riding ponies with very straight shoulders that cause a risk of the saddle slipping forward.

A crupper is also usually part of breaking tackle, though for young horses a crupper should have a buckle so that the tail does not have to be stuffed through the loop!

CURB. A swelling below the point of the hock brought about by strain or general weakness. It can sometimes be cured with rest or different shoeing and perhaps blistering. In severe cases the veterinarian may have to fire the lump (*q.v.*).

A curb is an unsoundness. It is easy to detect if the flat of the hand is run from the point of the hock down the leg.

CURB CHAIN. The length of chain which lies around the horse's lower jaw and which applies the leverage to the curb bit. These chains *must* lie flat to prevent rubbing sores.

DAISY CUTTER. A horse whose action is too low to the ground.

DALES PONY. A British-bred pony found in Yorkshire and

other northern parts.

They are small, active and reach 14.2 hands. Their colours are brown, grey and black. Chestnut is very rare. They have hairy heels, sloping quarters and plenty of bone. As they are docile and easy to break they are ideal for harness as well as saddle.

DAPPLED. Greys are often dappled. The grey colour is lighter or darker than the main colouring. Sometimes this second colour is in small circles.

DARK HORSE. Used as a reference to a race horse whose form is unknown.

DARTMOOR PONY. A very ancient breed of British pony found on Dartmoor. Their size should not exceed twelve hands and they are usually dark brown or bay. They have very good bone and action, a small head, sloping shoulders and a well set-on tail.

They are tough, strong little animals, very sure-footed and they easily survive the rugged Dartmoor winter weather.

They have lovable, cheeky faces and make splendid riding ponies for children but unfortunately the species may now be endangered.

DEALER. One who makes his living by buying and selling horses.

DEAD BEAT. A horse that is 'pumped': tired out, finished.

DEAD MEAT. A race horse whose stables know it cannot win because they have no intention of allowing this to happen! Very illegal.

DEATH. The physical signs of death are well known but there are times when these can be confusing; is the animal dead or not? It has been known for apparently dead foals to be taken from the mare and placed outside in the fresh air which, especially if cold, has suddenly revived them.

It is said that when the heart stops life ceases but this is not entirely accurate. There may still be electrical impulses in the brain. The best way to check is to try and find a heart beat, press a finger tip against an eye ball to see if it moves, and apply a mirror to the nostrils to see if it will mist over. If none of these tests produce a result, death may be presumed.

How do animals regard death?

We cannot know of course, but an observation of those dying, like domestic house pets, gives some indication that they do not view death as we do. A hunting animal understands death when it kills its prey. Its ability to attack and kill has ended something in another living creature but it is unreasonable to suppose it can view death as we humans would. This is one superior advantage over the animals which perhaps we could well do without – but I am *not* going to get involved in a religious debate in this book!

Perhaps death to them is merely a long sleep without hunger or pain? Something perfectly natural. Who knows? The writer certainly does not.

DELIVERY. The birth of the young.

DESTROY. The most humane way to destroy a horse or 'put him down' is to have him shot by the professional man with a humane killer.

DIAMOND SHOE. A shoe specially made for horses who 'forge' with their hind feet, or drag their toes. It is shaped like a playing-card diamond with the lower point missing.

DIARRHOEA or looseness of the bowel. Take this seriously and consult your veterinarian. This condition can be the indication of something more grave if it persists for more than a few hours.

DIGITALIS. This comes from the foxglove leaf gathered when the flowers are at a certain stage of growth, dried and used by both man and animal for heart conditions. Only ever to be used under the professional man's guidance – whether you have two legs or four.

DISINFECTANTS. They can be natural or factory produced. The very best, though, comes from leaving the stable door open to sun, wind and fresh air. After illness this is really important and, with the veterinarian's advice, also use a strong liquid chemical on the floors, walls and other surfaces. Good, well-run stables at all times swill their floors once a week with a mild disinfectant. There is absolutely no need for a stable to smell like one – so don't overdo it and make the box into a hospital!

DISMOUNT. To vacate the saddle – sometimes done with the horse's pugnacious assistance!

DISTANCE. When a race horse has won by more than twenty lengths.

DOCK. The bone of the tail.

DOCKING. A fiendish practice now banned by law. Men used to cut horses' tails for stupid fashion or because they thought the animal might take fright if its tail caught in the harness. The cruelty suffered in a hot summer when the poor animals were pestered with flies and had no tail to swish for protection must have driven many an animal half-crazy.

DON. A Russian breed of saddle horse. Tall, good-looking and fast. Excellent riding animals.

DONE. An exhausted animal. Also one whose grooming has been completed.

DONKEY. See ASS.

DOUBLE BRIDLE. A bridle composed of a bridoon and curb bit ridden with two reins in each hand. See also BITS.

DRAINAGE. Stable drainage must be adequate for the job. A central channel should lead to a mains drain well outside and away from the stable block.

There is no need for any stable to smell offensive!

DRAW. The racing position for some Starts is decided by a draw-like drawing out of a hat. Low numbers are usually on the left.

DRENCHING. To make a horse drink medicine by force. Absolutely essential when an exact dose of medicine is to be given. Hold the horse very firmly, open his mouth by extracting his tongue, place the bottle in the corner of the animal's mouth with the head well raised, and pour – *a little at a time!* Don't drown the poor animal! Give him time to swallow and catch his breath. A firm, knowledgeable assistant is always required. Horses like children, object to their medicine!

DRESSAGE. A form of horsemanship which, when polished, makes the animal a delightful and handy ride. The aids are highly skilled, require constant practice on the part of both man and animal and also involve certain Haute École movements.

DROP NOSEBAND. A nose band which closes the animal's mouth and jaws, stopping him from pulling. It must be fitted with extreme care under the bit and *not* above as with the ordinary noseband. Take great care that it does not impede the animal's breathing. A more popular noseband today is a Flash, the centre part of which is attached to the standard noseband. Once again, it must be fitted correctly.

DUN. A funny pale yellow-brown colour not unlike sand,

There is sometimes a black stripe on the back of the withers to tail.

DUNG. This is the colloquial name for the waste expelled by the body; the more correct word is faeces. In humans it is excreta.

Horses have the remarkable capacity to dung at any pace and even at speed; the exact opposite of the human race who must perform with quiet concentration.

Horse dung, if the animal is fit and healthy, is brown in colour and, because the horse is completely herbivorous, the odour is not unpleasant. The dung should be expelled in round balls, about the size of a golf ball. When it is other than this, feel alarm and stand by to call your vet. The body's waste is as valuable as a thermometer for indicating whether a problem is about to rear its ugly head.

Food enters the body by the mouth and comes out of the anus. In between, it goes down the gullet, into the stomach then starts a long journey along the intestines, sometimes called the guts. During this process, the goodness is extracted and that not required by the body is squeezed along, with muscular contractions, to be expelled as dung. Perfect for the garden!

The length of the horse's small intestine is about 70 feet and that of the large intestine roughly another 25 feet. This seems an enormous length but your own guts are about 28 feet!

Always keep an eye on your horse's dung. The round balls, as described above, often break upon hitting the ground which will give you the opportunity to examine them and see if any food appears. If this is so, ask why? It's abnormal and might indicate trouble with the teeth or the stomach.

Dung is not a topic of conversation for high society gatherings but it is of great importance nevertheless!

EMPLOYMENT. Those people who wish to work with horses, must be of a certain species! Obviously they must love the horse with all his foibles. They must be fit and have above average strength because there is a lot of lifting and heaving involved with food and bedding. They must also realise that involvement with horses is always a bit of a risk.

The types of stables for which employment will be available range from:

> Riding Schools
> Polo Stables
> Hunting Stables
> Competition Stables
> Racing Stables
> Livery Stables
to Private Stables
> Trekking Centres
and Holiday Hotels

All of the above need special requirements. For example, in Riding Schools where one teaches, qualifications are needed (see QUALIFICATIONS) and these can also be useful in other stables. They show aptitude, a few brains and lead to higher salaries.

Racing Stables only employ young people of a certain weight, especially those with flat race horses.

With a private stable, the groom will be in sole charge so his or her knowledge should cover the whole spectrum if possible. In larger stables, there will always be the old-fashioned stud groom or stable manager.

The hours can be long – very long – in hunting stables and you certainly will not get rich on the salary offered. On the other hand, job satisfaction is priceless and perhaps you will think that money is *not* everything after all.

When ready to seek work, study the columns of the *Horse and Hound* but, first of all, make sure you know exactly which type of stables you wish to work in.

ENCEPHALOMYELITIS. See ZOONOSES.

ENTIRE. An uncastrated male horse over the age of four years who has not been used for breeding.

EPIZOOTIC LYMPHANGITIS. A very contagious disease found in various parts of the world. It was unknown in the British Isles until horses returned from South Africa at the end of the Boer War. This disease may lie dormant for a long time; it is notifiable.

The infection usually starts from a wound and spreads like a bush fire. Tumours form and burst their contents. The animal must be destroyed and the police informed.

Fortunately, it is rare if not quite unknown now in the British Isles.

EXERCISE. Much the same as people take – or should take! Walking, trotting, cantering and galloping are the basic parts, though the actual work given to a horse depends upon the purpose. The racing animal will receive far more steady, hard work than the hunter and, in turn, the hunter gets more consistent work than the hack. Every living thing requires exercise. A fat, soft horse is every bit as useless as its human counterpart!

EXMOOR PONY. A famous British pony found on Exmoor which makes the perfect child's hunter. They are delightful little creatures and grow up to about 12.2 hands. Their colours are black, bay and dun with beautiful tan noses. There are no chestnuts. The head is sharp with a wide forehead, large nostrils, a little feather on the heels and a cheeky nature. They have lots of quality and character.

EXTENDED. A gait at full stretch, i.e. the extended trot not breaking into a canter, and the extended canter not quite a gallop.

FARRIER. A man or woman who has undergone a long apprenticeship and passed examinations enabling them to set up in business, shoeing horses.

Good farriers are worth their weight in gold and they are, even today, thin on the ground because shoeing horses is not without intense physical labour and more than a little risk. Especially from the horse's rear end.

Many of today's farriers travel around to stables, shoeing horses. They have small portable but highly efficient forges. They take with them rods of iron as well as shoes of various sizes because the skilled farrier makes the shoe fit the hoof and *not* the other way round.

Farriers also have the skills to provide remedial work on a damaged or diseased hoof. They can pare a hoof and provide special shoes for various conditions on a vet's recommendation, and most of them are likewise conversant with general equine ailments appertaining to the horse's legs, particularly the bones of the fetlock and pastern which work in conjunction with the few bones in the foot (see SHOEING).

FAULT. Something very much wrong with the animal; something amiss in his conformation.

FAVOURING. A horse 'favours' a lame leg by placing weight on the sound one instead. In simple terms – he limps!

47

FEAR. After love, fear is the greatest emotion for man or beast. Any man who says he doesn't know what fear is, is either stupid or remarkably brave. Usually though, he is the former! Every hero feels fear.

Animals know, by instinct, what man usually has to learn, that after fear comes another great emotion, anger! Animals and particularly horses will react to the person who shows fear of them. The animal *knows* that the man's next reaction will be anger so tries to 'get one in first'. Do you blame him? I don't! It stands to reason that if a person fears a horse then he should keep well away and try not to be a false hero. He'll only come off worse!

To attempt to handle a temperamental horse when in a state of fear is an action of reckless folly. There is nothing to be ashamed of in being afraid of a particular horse. It's far more honest – and courageous – to admit the fear and retreat than blunder in like an idiot.

Fear, though, should be overcome if possible. If this is not possible don't have anything to do with that horse. Ride another! When a horse has a 'mood on' he can be very frightening indeed!

FEATHER. This is the long hair below the knees and round the fetlock joints of animals that are 'cold blooded' (not well bred) and heavy horses as well as some ponies. Well-bred horses have little feather.

With heavy horses like the Shire or Clydesdale, feather is expected and admired.

FEEDING. Nature made the horse to spend his days ambling across long, grassy plains nibbling away at his leisure. She gave him a small stomach. Therefore, feed little and often. For the stabled, worked horse, four feeds a day with a hay net morning and night and constant fresh water is enough to keep the horse happy and content. The quantity a horse requires depends upon the amount and type of work done.

Some horses are good eaters. They will even eat their clothing if of that mind! Others, like children, have to be tempted, so deal with each animal according to his temperament. Don't try to use a set of rules for each animal indiscriminately or you will soon be in trouble!

When obtaining a new horse always find out from the last owner what the animal's eating habits were. It saves a lot of work and worry. Remember, veterinarian's bills are expensive. That poor man has to eat too!

FELL PONY. A British native pony found in the north of the country. He should not grow more than 14.2 hands and should be strong, agile and sure-footed.

Fells make good children's ponies though they lack a bit of quality. They should have thick manes and some feather at the heels which can make them look a little common. Their colours are black, brown with a few greys.

FETLOCK. The joint above the pastern.

FILLY. A young female who has not been used for breeding.

FIRE. All living creatures are terrified of fire, with good reason. The downright terror of a horse trapped in a stable cannot be imagined.

'No smoking' should be an iron clad rule, rigorously enforced, in all areas connected with stables. Many of the items used with horses are of a highly inflammable nature, especially hay and straw.

Spend some money to install fire extinguishers, and know how to use them. If in doubt as to the exact chemicals to be poured into these extinguishers, get

49

advice from the local Fire Brigade. It is no bad rule to have plenty of buckets of water placed at strategic points. Make sure all electrical points are properly wired and 100% safe.

Do not allow yourself to become complacent where fire is concerned. Remember the horse, locked in the stable with a firmly bolted door, cannot let himself out!

FIRED. An animal whose legs have been fired for the operation of removing splints or curbs. This operation leaves distinct scars.

There is pin-firing and bar-firing. In pin-firing the veterinarian fires straight into the cause of the trouble but with bar-firing he works in lines. These leave the scars. The object of firing is to shatter the cause of the trouble – lameness – with extensive and concentrated heat. Splints are usually pin-fired, curbs usually bar-fired.

FLAT. Flat races where a horse does not jump.

Racing is as much an instinct with horses as it is with men.

It is thought that ancient Arabia was the home of riding so it is also considered to be the birthplace of racing. One of the early – savage – methods of making horses race was to keep them very short of water for some time and then let them out for a drink.

Before the Roman invasion of Britain riding was not very common but the native ponies were used in chariots and chariot races were popular.

Racing really started in Britain about AD 4 when Arabians were run.

The Anglo-Saxons loved a horse race.

The name of the first proper British race horse was that of a stallion called Arundel owned by Sir Bevys of Hampton.

Racing was popular under Richard I and Richard II; then it sank into decline. This accelerated under Henry VIII who, because of his great weight and that of the armour then in use, insisted all horses should be weight carriers. In the reign of Elizabeth I racing slowly started to expand again. James I bred horses for racing on a very large scale and he also started races at Newmarket. Charles I was devoted to racing horses and even the puritan Oliver Cromwell adored a horse race. Queen Anne founded Ascot in 1712 and in 1756 the Jockey Club was formed. The 12th Earl of Derby founded the Derby and Oaks races in 1780 while Col. St Leger inaugurated the race bearing his name in 1776. Racing flourished in the nineteenth century. Today it is more than a sport; it is big business.

Flat races are run over various distances, some with handicaps. The prize money is good, the rewards very worthwhile. The sport, as a whole, is vastly popular the world over.

FLEMISH. A heavy, rather common looking animal from Europe.

FLEXIONS. Movements made by the reins which command the horse. The animal bends his head at the poll, gives with his jaw and moves in the required direction (see AIDS).

FOAL. A baby horse.

FOOT. A most complex subject. The saying 'no foot, no hoss!' is so true! A horse's foot comprises only a few bones: the pedal or coffin bone, the navicular, the short pastern bone and the end of the long pastern bone. The horn can be compared to the human nail. One of the most important and highly sensitive parts of the hoof is the frog. This is nature's shock absorber and cushion.

Only a skilled farrier should ever deal with the foot. If

you suspect foot lameness get the professional in without hesitation.

FORAGE. The trade name for horse food, i.e. hay, oats, etc.

FORE. The front leg, as hind means the rear, i.e. the near fore leg is the left front leg.

FOREHAND. All that part in front of the saddle.

FORELOCK. The hair between the ears which hangs down the forehead.

FORGING. When a horse is tired or clumsy or just has a bad gait he drags his toes. This is a tiresome and bad habit which should be corrected by instant collection. If the gait is at fault, though, get the farrier to put on special shoes.

FORWARD SEAT. The seat used for jumping. The idea is to get the rider's weight out of the saddle and off the loins and kidneys. Sit forward, have the hands low on each side of the horse's neck and grip well.

In olden days riders had the curious idea that the weight should go backwards for jumping! Thus, at the most crucial moment, they put considerable strain on the tender loins.

FOXY OATS. These are oats that have become wet or germinated. The well fed horse will refuse them; the starving one will bolt them with disastrous results. There will be diarrhoea, which can be severe. After a horse eats foxy oats it is rare for death to occur but it is not unknown.

FRACTURES. Breaks in bones which come, as with people, in varying degrees of severity. Any fracture in a horse must be treated very seriously. Because of the animal's size it is often necessary to destroy it but only the veterinarian can make this decision, always bearing in mind the cost of the pain to the animal.

FROG. A portion of the foot. When the foot is lifted a V-shaped cleft is to be seen. This is the frog: the shock absorber, the cushion. Sometimes stones may lodge in the grooves of the V and these should be removed immediately and with care. Always leave the frog alone. Do not go paring it with a knife. No farrier worth his salt will touch the frog.

FRONT. A horse has a good front when there is plenty of room before the saddle with a good, sloping shoulder.

FULL MOUTH. A horse of six years with a full mouth has all his teeth.

FUNK. A temperamental horse who works himself into a tizzy over nothing!

GAIT. A horse's pace. There are four main gaits, i.e. the walk, trot, canter and gallop. In some countries though there is a fifth, known as a triple or run. This gait is like an ambling trot and a horse can cover vast distances without tiring. Many Icelandic ponies are trained to acquire this gait.

GALL. A skin sore caused by constant chafing. Usually found around the girth near the elbows when a soft or young horse has been saddled too young or too carelessly.

Bath the gall, then dust it with antiseptic powder. If the animal must still be used, pad the offending leather with some soft material until the skin toughens.

GALLOP. The fastest pace. A well-bred highly-trained race horse can usually reach 30-34 m.p.h.

GALLOWAY. A pony breed from the north of Britain that is not at all common. The animal stands up to fourteen hands.

GARRON. The Scottish Garron, from the Highlands, is a heavy, strong, useful animal but over the years he has lost many of his 'pony' characteristics. These ponies are most used now for carrying packs and loads over the mountains.

They grow to fifteen hands and come in nearly all colours except chestnut.

GASKIN. The thigh of the hindleg.

GATE. The barrier used at the start of races.

GAY. Describes a horse who carries his head high, who walks with pride and who, in general, considers life to be very good indeed. Often requires the rider to have a tight grip!

GELDING. A castrated male horse.

GENEROUS. A kind, obedient horse who responds willingly to every command and who does not spare himself.

GIRTH. The strap of leather or other strong material which holds the saddle in position. It should be kept scrupulously clean and supple. Always pay attention to the buckles to make sure they are sound and quite strong.

The thoughtful rider always makes sure that the animal's skin is not 'puckered' under the girth, causing pain.

Girth is also used as a term when referring to the circumference of the horse's body.

GLANDERS. A serious, contagious disease which can be passed to man and is therefore classed as a Notifiable Disease.

Glanders' signs are so varied that only a professional can diagnose correctly; he symptoms are often similar to those of Strangles and even indeed the common cold.

Glanders has been known since the days of Hippocrates and has appeared in nearly every country in the world. It is caused by a most dangerous bacillus and the most common way of infection seems to be by skin contact.

Farcy is often read of in connection with Glanders and usually refers to the dreadful running sores which arise with this disease. There is little treatment. The law states that the animal must be destroyed.

GLEET. A discharge from the horse's nostrils with a bad smell. Skilled treatment is necessary. This can sometimes be confused with Glanders.

GOES WELL. An expression for a horse who jumps and gallops freely.

GOOD REIN. This means the horse has a nice, big front with room for plenty of rein between the bit and the hands.

GOOSE RUMPED. A conformation fault when the tail is set on too low and the quarters droop. There is also an arch where the tail starts.

GRASS. Grass is more than the stuff you chop level with the lawn mower. It is the horse's natural food and, in Britain, may also be referred to as pasture or pastureland for stock.

There are many types of grasses which vary, in horse quality, from the good to the poor and it is a wise owner who makes a study of their good points to compare against the bad ones. Some of the good nutritious grasses are Timothy, Italian ryegrass, perennial ryegrass, ryegrass and both meadow and red fescue. The rough-stalked meadowgrass and the more smooth variety are also excellent.

Those which come under the heading of merely fair or poor are the white clover, sheep's fescue, cocksfoot, bent and Yorkshire fog. As hay is nothing but dried grass for the horse's winter feeding, it is always prudent to try and find out from where the grass was cut to make the hay.

It is simply useless to feed a horse grass which is only of a fair quality because he cannot be expected to thrive as well as the animal fed upon a better variety.

So make a point of looking at grasses as you go out and

GRASSES: *Top, left to right*: White clover, Bent.
Middle: Sheeps fescue. *Foot*: Yorkshire fog, Cocksfoot

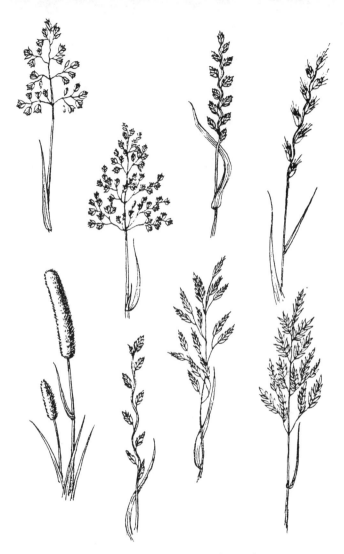

Top line: Smooth meadow grass, Rough meadow grass, Italian rye, Rye grass. *Bottom line*: Timothy grass, Perennial rye, Meadow fescue, Red fescue.

about, fixing in your mind and eye those which you know your horse should eat.

GRASS CUTTINGS. Lawnmower and other machine grass cuttings are not a food to give to horses because they can ferment in the stomach and start colic.

GRASS SICKNESS. A disease of unknown cause which attacks animals during May, June and July. In the British Isles it seems to occur a lot in Scotland and the West coastal regions. There is thought to be a connecting link between the time of the year and the juice of the clover when the plant is growing strongly.

The horse loses his appetite, becomes dull, acquires a discharge at the nostrils and suffers from an internal blockage. He grows weak and then usually dies.

There is no satisfactory cure. Two varieties of the disease occur and some horses do recover after an attack of the Sub-acute variety but they are weak for a long time.

GRAZING. Good grass land which should ideally have running water and shelter against hot sun or cold wind.

GREASE. A fetlock condition often caused by the horse standing in continually wet, filthy conditions though Grease can also appear in healthy horses. The symptoms are swelling, redness and itching. Get help at once. See MUD FEVER.

GREEN. Describes a young, unschooled horse who has been broken to the saddle but not taught the aids or manners of any kind.

GREY. A colour which ranges from white and cream to dun. White hairs are present on the body and legs intermixed with light or darker hair in various shades of grey.

GRIP. The rider's grip should be from the knee and thigh using all the muscles of the inside leg, including those at the groin going into the abdomen.

GROOM. A person whose work comprises looking after horses. A highly skilled job requiring study, knowledge, experience and dedication.

GROOMING. Attending to the horse's toilet, i.e. his appearance! Good grooming, by hand, is very hard work which should produce a lather of sweat on the groomer! It is essential for the stabled horse's health. It tones up both skin and muscle with the action of the brush. The wisp acts as a massage.

The horse should be brushed lightly with the dandy brush then worked very hard, all over, with the body brush which is cleaned with the metal comb. Do not use the comb on the horse! Wisp vigorously then finish off with a clean cloth.

The easiest thing to do, though, in this Moon Age is to buy electrical grooming equipment. It is effective and most animals take kindly to it. It also saves the groom an awful lot of sweating!

GROUND HITCHED. The action when the reins are left lying on the ground and the horse stands without moving. All American Western horses are taught this and it has often baffled the writer why this simple education is omitted from British horses' tuition.

GRUNTING UNDER THE STICK. A rough test for broken wind. Pretend to hit the horse in the ribs with fist or stick. If he flinches and grunts noisily, suspect the worse!

HACK. A horse used solely for pleasure riding as opposed to the hunter and race horse which are bred for specific jobs.

A well-trained hack should answer to all the aids and

should be a pleasant, comfortable ride at all paces. Hacks are of no set breeding but an Arab crossed with a Thoroughbred or half-bred makes a good animal for pleasure riding.

HACKAMORE. A bitless bridle which relies for control on nasal pressure. Very useful for the animal with an injured mouth or one whose mouth has been ruined.

HACKNEY. A high-stepping harness horse standing about fifteen hands. It probably originated as a cross between local trotting mares and an Arabian import.

Bay is the most common colour but the odd black and grey are found.

They are quite perfect horses for pulling a light chaise or trap but with their high-stepping gait they are a wickedly uncomfortable ride!

HAFFLINGER. A pony of cobby looks, standing about fourteen hands, found in Austria. It has the palomino colouring with powerful quarters and legs that show a lot of feather.

HALF BRED. An animal with one Thoroughbred parent or one parent that is full-bred of the breed in question.

HALTER. Made from rope. It fits over the head and nose without a bit. It is used for leading or tying an animal.

HAMSTRUNG. When a major tendon has been cut and the limb hangs uselessly. The animal has to be put down.

HAND. An equine measurement which equals four inches, 10 cms.

HANDICAP. In racing, handicappping is the attempt to give horses an equal chance. Their past form and proven abilities are taken into account, their jockeys and sadles weighed, and the handicapped onces made to carry extra weight.

The weights are of particular importance in a long, arduous race like The Grand National.

HANDLED. A horse who has become used to people being around and to them touching or handling him but who has not yet been broken.

HANDS. They say these are born and not made but the writer thinks they can be acquired. It is certainly true that some riders will never produce the gentle hands needed for sympathetic communication with the horse's mouth – just as some people are a menace in a china shop!

Good hands are strong, kind, firm and understanding.

HAND SALE. This is a sale where there is nothing in writing. It is a 'gentleman's agreement', both seller and buyer agreeing on the price and sealing the bargain with a handshake. Not the most satisfactory way of doing business!

In the north of the British Isles there is another type of

hand sale. The seller gives his price and extends his hand. If the buyer disagrees he knocks the hand aside, names his offer then shows his hand. This knocking aside of hands and fresh offers continue until agreement is finally reached. A dubious way of commerce!

HARDY. Describes a tough horse of rugged body who lives outdoors in all weathers yet who is never sick or sorry.

HARNESS. The equipment a horse wears when pulling. This comprises bridle, bit and reins, collar, hames and traces, backpad, pad and crupper. All should be kept oiled or soaped, soft and supple.

HAUTE ÉCOLE. The name of advanced training in the aids. They include many specific movements and controlled jumps in the air, marking time on the spot and other elaborate evolutions.

Some people are inclined to despise Haute École and ask what use it performs, but education never hurt either man or beast. Much of the training, the writer agrees, cannot be used in general riding but many of the movements go back in history and have their reasons.

The Spanish Riding School of Vienna is famous worldwide for its displays given on its Lipizzaner stallions. These horses seem most suited to this type of training and make a fabulous sight when in action.

Most of the movements are taught to the horse without a rider while the rider himself has to learn the necessary aids. Only when both man and animal are well versed in everything they are matched together. Many ordinary riders would be lost on a trained Lipizzaner.

A lot of equine circus acts derive their movements from the Haute École and these themselves go back into the mists of time and history when the mounted knight wanted his horse to fight as well as himself. The balanced rears with the striking front hooves, the leap in the air with the hind legs kicking outwards, the marching on the spot to confuse an enemy – all were invented for a specific purpose and have come down to us now as Haute École and entertainment. See SPANISH RIDING SCHOOL OF VIENNA.

HAY. Dried grass: the horse's basic food. It can be likened to man's need for bread.

The best is called seed hay and is rich with clover. New hay can cause looseness of the bowels – just as a freshly baked hot loaf can give stomach ache to a human being!

Hay should always smell sweet and be clean without any trace of dust or must. How much hay a horse requires depends entirely upon the horse and his personal habits.

The best way in which to give the hay is in a net suspended from high on the wall – though make sure that a hoof cannot get entangled if the horse is a vigorous eater and pulls his net loose. See GRASS.

HAYNET. A net made of thin rope fastened with a draw string into which the hay is placed. Some horses are extravagant and wasteful animals but with a net it is almost impossible for a horse to pull out too much at once and waste his hay by trampling on it.

HAY WISP. Gather tendrils of hay into a long 'string' by twisting and turning. Then when about two feet long, tie into a figure of eight. Use this then when grooming as a massage. Most (though not all) horses love being wisped and it gives a good shine to the coat. It stimulates the muscles and is greatly beneficial.

HEAD COLLAR. Made of strong leather, this slips over the

63

animal's head for wear on the head. A rope can be attached for leading purposes. If a horse is crafty to catch always turn him out with a head collar on. It saves an awful amount of human energy and temper!

HEEL BUG. A disease of the heels often caused by horses being out early in morning dampness. Race horses can acquire this if their heels are not dried properly after exercise in the first string. If the redness and soreness do not respond to dusting powders, get help. See MUD FEVER.

HIGH HEELS. At times, raised calkins are placed upon the hind shoes when the back tendons have been sprained but they should not be used for too long, otherwise the animal will never be able to do without them. See SHOEING.

HIGHLAND PONY. A Scottish native pony not quite so coarse as the Garron who stands between 13.2 and 14.2 hands high. They have attractive heads with bright, bold eyes and short ears.

Their colours are chiefly duns and greys. At times there is a dark stripe running down the back. They have a tuft of silky hair at the heels and are sure-footed and tough.

HIND. Meaning rear.

HINNY. The offspring from a female ass and a stallion.

HOBDAY. An operation performed by the veterinarian to cure wind trouble. An incision is made in the throat about two inches long and this leaves the identifying scar. Horses thus Hobdayed are supposed to be unable to whinny but the writer rode a Hobdayed horse who was anything but dumb!

The operation was made popular by Sir Frederick Hobday. It gives a high percentage of cures though considerable rest must be given to the animal after the operation for strength to be regained.

The horse has to be anaesthetised for this operation.

HOCK. The joint of the hind leg which roughly corresponds to man's ankle.

HOGGED MANE. A mane cut off entirely.

HONEST. A hard-working horse who plays no tricks.

HORSE. What is a horse? Such a question might seem stupid, but a thoughtful study of exactly what constitutes such an animal makes it easier to handle a horse and more enjoyable to ride one.

A horse is a social animal who, in the natural state, lives in a herd controlled and ruled by a dominant stallion. He looks after his mares, breeds them when they come into season, keeps an eye on the foals and then throws out the young males when he considers their presence no longer desirable.

He is the boss, although in a herd there is a pecking order among the mares with one who leads and sets an example and another poor unfortunate who is always at the tail end of the queue and who receives all the kicks and bites!

Never forget that even the strongest man is pretty puny compared to a fully grown horse. We only control them through the superior ability of our brain so a study of their natural behaviour never goes amiss.

Any horse's reaction to danger is to run away from it, so when your ridden horse shies at some dragon such as a piece of fluttering paper, he is only reacting as nature intended. What is it? Will it hurt? Run away from it just in case! The same applies to a cornered horse. If he cannot gallop away he will be left with one trump card: attack from feet and heels.

Watch your horse's face and his expressions. Body language plays an important part in horse behaviour especially from the highly expressive ears, uplifted head and staring eyes.

A horse can only act like a horse so it is up to you to meet him half way at least. Remember you are supposed to have the superior brain; prove it by how you handle your horse.

HORSE SICKNESS. Also known as African Horse Sickness. This disease is prevalent during the summer and is caused by a virus. There are four main types that all require veterinary treatment. The basic signs are a rise in the temperature, difficulty in breathing, considerable sweating and a cough with nasal discharge.

Complications may occur, such as blindness, and there is little that can be done. Vaccination is far more sensible than risking a horse's health.

HORSESHOE. See SHOEING.

HUMOUR. This does not mean the horse is going to clap his hooves at your current joke! – The word refers to small lumps which appear under the skin from too much rich living and not enough work. The blood becomes upset, just as yours would if you lived on cream cakes and stayed in bed all day. The term can refer to any fluid or collection of fluid in the body's tissues.

Consult your vet. Prevention is much easier than cure.

HUNTER. An animal bred and trained for hunting. He must be able to go a good gallop and be a safe jumper over all fixed and natural obstacles, as well as having stamina and soundness.

Arabs are too hot and excitable to make good hunters and Thoroughbreds can sometimes be a handful. The half bred is ideal as is the Anglo-Arab. Ireland produces excellent hunters.

HUNTER'S CERTIFICATE. No horse may race in a point to point unless a Hunter's Certificate has been lodged. This is to obviate the running of 'professional' horses in an amateur affair.

To obtain the certificate the owner must take the horse out hunting the requisite number of times and draw the Master's attention to this fact. No valuable race horse is going to be allowed to join in the hurly-burly of the hunting field though many do so after they have retired from racing.

HUNTING ACCIDENTS. These can be anything from a simple bruise or over-reach (*q.v.*) to a serious stake wound. Common sense should be used. Treat the animal as you would yourself. If it is serious get professional help.

ICELAND. This country has small, tough ponies not unlike Shetlands with attractive heads, bold eyes and small ears. They have thick manes, carry their tails well and are very strong.

INCUBATION. This is most important, whether one is a horse owner, groom or stable manager. It is vital to know the incubation period for disease especially when dealing with many horses in a yard. A sick animal must be removed and isolated but, more to the point, the contact horse must be located and identified if possible and also isolated.

Incubation is the time period between infection and the actual appearance of disease. Below are a few average times, though these may vary depending upon the horse, its age, location and a number of other factors.

Anthrax	12 to 24 hours or more
Glanders	1 to 6 weeks or more

Epizootic Lymphangitis	8 days to 9 months
Influenza	3 to 10 days
Strangles	3 to 8 days
Tetanus	4 days to 3 weeks
Variola or horse pox	6 to 8 days

A very rough rule of thumb is that the longer the period between infection and the disease appearing the milder the attack is likely to be. The shorter the period, the more virulent the disease.

Even when the disease has gone and the animal is better, it is always prudent to keep the horse apart from its fellows. Always follow the vet's instructions and practice strict hygiene whenever disease is present.

INFECTION. We all know what infection is when it affects us. It is the word we use to denote the spread of something either in the body itself or from an outside source. When this latter is by contact it is called contagious.

By either means, disease can travel from one animal to another and also from animal to man. When the latter it is called a Notifiable Disease and is covered by Statute, i.e. The Contagious Disease Act of Animals. Certain diseases must be reported to the authorities. See ZOONOSES.

Infection can also come from sources other than living ones. When it is so it is called Indirect Infection and can be transmitted through grooming tools, soiled bedding, animal clothing, human hands and dress, floors and walls, railway loose boxes and even the soil and vegetation.

Infection must never be treated lightly because it can be a forerunner of something lethal to either man or beast.

Germs may be classified into two separate branches: those which can only thrive in or on a living body, and others which live independently upon a dead body or foliage matter, even at a lower temperature. It is usual to expect the first group to be more serious than the latter although Anthrax is an exception as is Foot and Mouth disease and the recent BSE. In these diseases fire is the only way to eradicate the danger although Anthrax is known to linger for a long time like the Bubonic plagues which affected Britain in the Middle Ages.

Never be complacent with any type of infection. Get help and get it quickly. See also Isolation.

INFLAMMATION. The signs are exactly those which apply to man. Heat, redness, pain and swelling. The swelling is usually seen first; this is caused by the blood's action in fighting and resisting the cause. Use commonsense. Bathe with cold water to reduce swellings and hot water with an antiseptic for open wounds. Keep very clean. If there is pain get help. Remember, the horse is a very stoical animal. Because he doesn't yell for help don't think he can't suffer.

INFLUENZA. Also known as Pink Eye. This is, like the human version, highly contagious and the horse feels just as rotten as you when you get a bout of 'flu.

There are two types and it is the malignant one that is known as Pink Eye.

It attacks young horses a lot, spreads very rapidly, appearing with a lack of appetite, dullness and rising temperature. The pulse is fast, there is a nasal discharge and lots of shivering. If the reader has had 'flu − and who hasn't ? − the horse will suffer just like you.

Complications can arise. Neither man nor animal should treat 'flu lightly. You would quickly get yourself the doctor. Do the same for the horse.

INSURANCE. This is of vital importance today, especially Third Party and fully comprehensive. People are very quick to take legal action for real or imagined wrongs and there is an element of the population who regard riders as undesirables.

Insurance is imperative for your own purse. Veterinarian fees are steep because they too have to pay their bills and make a living. Do shop around for a suitable insurance though and make sure you understand what it is going to cost per month. Taking out insurance is no cheap game so it is prudent to discuss the matter with other horse owners. For goodness sake, do read all the small print before committing yourself!

Insurance must not just cover the horse and any damage or injury which might arise to a third party. It must protect you too! If you have a fall and are injured and have to take time off from work, what happens to your salary?

Riding is a risk game, without a doubt; even simple hacking, especially on the roads going from here to there. Most insurances, unfortunately, contain an Exclusion Clause and this one you must study in detail. Quite a few insist that you will have to pay the first £100 no matter what, and this clause may also extend to vets' bills.

It is critically important that both you, your horse and any other possible rider are fully covered for every conceivable eventuality. This will cost, but at least you will have peace of mind when you hack or hunt out.

INTELLIGENCE. There has been a lot of rubbish aired about a horse's intelligence compared to other domestic animals and pets. It has been argued that if a horse lived in a home, like a cat or dog, he too would demonstrate his proven intelligence through his social intercourse with man. It is a fine point but *non proven* as the Scots would say in their courts.

Examining the size of the brain, per body weight, it is seen that the horse does come after the cat and dog; the former of which, as it happens, is deemed not too bright simply because of its natural independence from man. Perhaps it is a case of handsome is as handsome does!

Haute École and Circus horses can and do learn complicated tricks but that is through repetition and rote. It does not come from figuring the said tricks out for themselves.

Every living creature can only advance as far as its brain permits which, in turn, depends upon the proportions of grey and white matter. The cerebrum and the highly complex nerve processes in the cerebrum also figure highly in the intelligence stakes.

What is positive is that one 'cannot make a silk purse from a sow's ear.'

IRISH. A horse bred in Ireland.

These animals make first-class hunters; race horses also do well in that country. They breed them with big bone and much substance.

The weather conditions in Ireland are particularly suitable for horse breeding, owing to the considerable amount of limestone and the wet climate which makes such excellent grass.

IRON. The name for the stirrup.

ISABELLA. A colour which refers to Queen Isabella of Spain and a favourite breed of horse. We now know this as Palomino.

ISOLATION. To prevent the spread of disease, isolate the horse that is sick. Let only one person attend to the animal and make him or her practise hygiene.

JADEY. A horse who has lost his condition, lost his spirit and, in general, feels as if the end of the world has come!

JAGGER. An ancient name for the pack horse.

JANET. A female mule.

JENNET. A small Spanish horse.

JENNY. A female ass.

JIBBING. An objection on the horse's part to doing something when ordered – like jumping a fence. It often starts out as mischief or plain cussedness but can develop into a vice unless checked.

A large number of horses start jibbing through fright and they can quickly go from bad to worse.

If fright is the cause, the rider must patiently overcome the animal's fear. If the horse jibs from awkwardness then he must be made to face up to the obstacle.

If he jibs otherwise, it might be because some part of his tack is hurting. He can't tell you; he should not have to! Man is supposed to have the better brain.

If your horse jibs for no reason, look around and find out if there is anything wrong.

JOB. A savage snatch at the horse's mouth causing him pain and fright. An unforgivable action. Never punish a horse this way.

JOB HORSE. An old name for a worn-out carriage horse who was hired or jobbed out for the day.

JOCKEY. A person who rides race horses for his living with a licence.

JOCKEY CLUB. Founded in 1756. The law and authority for flat racing in Britain. Most countries have a Jockey Club based upon the British version.

JODHPURS. A version of riding trousers which are flared

at the thigh and go down to the ankle. They originated in India.

JOINT. This is the union of bones and the most common joint giving trouble is the fetlock and hock.

JOINT ILL. This disease occurs mostly in foals just after birth when the unhealed naval cord assimilates germs which travel into the foal's blood.

Strict hygiene is necessary with both mare and foal at birth but it is not easy to render a stable sterile.

The foal's joints swell, the animal becomes dull and refuses to suckle. A nasty abscess appears at the umbilical cord. Get help at once!

JUMPER. An animal whose speciality is jumping over fences either when racing or at shows.

A natural jumper has big quarters and powerful hocks with plenty of spring and 'go' in him.

KATHIAWARI. This horse can be considered indigenous to the Indian Continent and its suspected origin, like so

many others, is that of the Arab.

It is a tough, hardy but narrow horse and sometimes has a high tail carriage like an Arab. It does have one rather remarkable physical characteristic. It has very long ears which turn inwards at their tips until they almost touch. These horses stand about fifteen hands but often have weak hindquarters and hind legs without strength, but it makes quite a nice riding animal with a fair degree of intelligence.

KICKER. An animal who kicks is dangerous to himself and any other living creature in the vicinity of the hind hoofs.

Kicking is a vice and a most difficult one to break − if not impossible. Horses that kick should wear a red ribbon around the tail.

Always approach a strange horse with caution and respect in case it kicks. It must be remembered that nature gave the horse a highly strung nervous system with quick reflexes and a defence of kick first and question later! See VICE.

KINETON NOSEBAND. A noseband for pullers; it requires careful adjustment as it works in conjunction with the snaffle bit looped around the bit bar.

KNACKER. One who disposes of horses' dead bodies.

KNUCKLING OVER. A condition sometimes seen in old, overworked animals where the fetlock joint knuckles over and the limb shakes. It can sometimes be known as Overshot Fetlocks. There is not very much even the veterinarian can do with this condition.

LAMENESS. Lameness and the cause is a subject vast enough to warrant its own book. Many are the causes of lameness, some minor, others serious. A few are: splints, sprains, bruises, curbs, throughpins, spavins, sidebones, ringbones, as well as disease.

Whenever lameness appears it is always wise to consult your veterinarian.

To find out which foot is lame when the cause is not immediately apparent from the effect, such as a limb resting unnaturally, trot the horse out on a long rein; watch his head from front and rear. You should see him nod his head in time to the action of the lame leg.

Lameness can also be felt with the hand seeking out heat or swelling, or both. Also study the animal's face. He will flinch when hurt, just like you. He won't yell, though!

LAMINITIS. A disease of which its cause is not fully understood. It may arise from a number of factors. A horse and especially a greedy pony without enough work can over eat grass.

General unfit conditions can also start this disease.

Incorrect shoeing with too much hard road work is another possible factor but diet is often the culprit. A diet with too high protein and too little work can start the problem.

There is an inflammation of the hoof, and it must be remembered that the few bones of the hoof are enclosed in a solid box, so if swelling starts there is nowhere for it to go. It causes raised body temperature, rapid breathing and much pain; the horse's expression will tell you this, although long before the agony becomes clear you should have called in the vet. This is a serious condition and requires immediate professional consultation.

LAMPAS. A mouth and palate condition that sometimes comes when teeth are being cut. Obtain professional advice; how would you like it if your toothache was to be dealt with by the plumber?

LANCERS BIT. A severe curb bit ridden with double reins, and not for learners! This was once used a lot by polo players.

LARYNX. A condition and/or illness of the respiratory system, the first symptom of which is usually a cough or two. A session of coughing can be a sign of something more sinister so get your vet straight away. The diseases which affect this part of the body include whistling, roaring and bronchitis. They also can be a pointer to something else, and only the vet can investigate with certainty.

LAW, THE, This is a highly complex subject best left to your family solicitor – if he knows horses, that is!

Many acts have gone on to the statute books relating to other animals besides horses; some in the last century have been repealed with new ones added.

Always remember when riding your horse that you might be responsible for a Litigation claim if your horse should shy, kick and damage, say, a car which had stopped, with engine off, to allow you to pass.

If you buy a horse and, after a period, find the animal does not match the sale description, are you prepared to go to Law? It can be a hideously expensive business as well as time consuming.

Where do you stand if your horse escapes from its field, trespasses, and does damage to another's property?

What is your legal responsibility if, say, you allow a minor to ride and exercise your horse and he/she is thrown and is hurt or even seriously injured?

What if, when riding in company, your £500 pony has a rush of blood to its head and kicks and permanently wounds and lames another's £5,000 hunter? Who is going to pay the hunter's vet's bills?

Consider insurance, and go into it very thoroughly, making sure you read all the small print. It does no harm to have a quiet word with your solicitor who knows how many horse beans make five!

LEADERS. Tendons.

LEADING A HORSE. The horse should not be allowed to trail behind the person nor should he be allowed to rush ahead. He should walk at your elbow where he is most under control.

Strictly speaking, when a rider leads a horse he should do so on the right and on that side of the road, but with today's present-day traffic conditions this can be a very worrying situation. In countries which drive on the right the position should be reversed. Use common sense. Make allowances for cars being driven fast round corners.

LEASING & **LOANING**. This can be fraught with peril so DIY efforts are not advised. Use your horsey solicitor.

Inspect the stables first of all and see their standards. Eye up the staff, too, and run a careful eye over the condition of the tack in the saddle room and the locale of all food and hay. Are these areas clean and free of rodents? What fire precautions are there? What about security?

There must be a clear, written understanding of who pays what and for how long. Note that there is a huge difference between a Lease and a Loan. If you value your animal – and who does not? – then go into everything from the thread to the needle.

There must be absolute clarity about who is to ride the horse and under what conditions.

Do *not*, under any circumstances, try to save money by arranging all this yourself.

LEATHERS. From leathers hang the stirrups. They are

made of thick, strong leather which should be kept clean and well soaped. They hang from the saddle bar.

LEG-UP. To be assisted into the saddle the rider lifts up the left leg and is tossed or legged-up into the saddle.

LEVADE. An Haute École movement where the horse rises on its hindlegs and maintains its balance.

LIGHTING. Horses require adequate lighting, preferably natural, in their stables.

LINSEED. A grain full of oil. This should be soaked and boiled before being given in the form of a mash. It should be boiled until it jells. It is rich and tasty to the tired horse.

LIPIZZANER. A grey horse who is used extensively in Haute École at the Spanish Riding School of Vienna.

LISK. The horse's groin.

LIVERPOOL HORSE. One who appears capable of jumping the tough Aintree Steeplechasing course in the Grand National.

LIVERY. This means that your horse is boarded out with other people in their stables.

Liveries vary. There is full livery when only you ride the horse and all is found for the animal: bedding, food and all forage. Vet's bills might be the subject of negotiation as will farrier's bills.

Under part livery someone else is allowed to ride the horse and the owner pays less money. This needs going into thoroughly, especially if the horse is liveried at a riding stables. – Who is to be allowed to ride your horse and when?

With DIY livery you just pay for the stable and do everything else yourself. Not only do you look after the horse but you provide all forage and fodder as well as bedding. Only you ride the horse.

When putting a horse out to livery it is critically important that all the above details are made very clear and it is better if this is done in writing. It can save many arguments in the long run!

LOCK JAW. The common name for Tetanus (*q.v.*).

LONG DISTANCE RIDING. This is great fun though heaven help the rider who does not have a fit bottom!

It is a competitive sport which is exceedingly tough for man and beast. If a rider has the temperament for the roar and applause of the crowds, then it is not for him because distance riding can be lonely. When the terrain and weather get tough, company is greatly desired by both two legs and four.

There are differing levels and distances though the beginner should attempt only an unranked endurance test.

The minimum distance is about 19 miles while it is 99 miles for the large events. The horse is examined by a vet before the ride commences and there are regular spot veterinary checks along the way.

Some distance riding feats are against the clock, one of the highest speeds of which is 4, which means about 9 miles per hour with distances from 19 to 50 miles.

There are penalty points for being late though nothing is to be gained by arriving early, so some clever watch-spotting and distance-reading ability is required by the rider. At all times, the rider must not reach a check point with a distressed horse.

It is thought that one of the best horses for this discipline is the Arab who has great, natural endurance, though perhaps such an animal is not the most comfortable to ride for long periods. What is needed is absolute, peak fitness on the part of man and mount. Anything less and the horse is disqualified. The rider? – He could well end up a hospital case because saddle sores are agony.

LONG IN THE TOOTH. An old horse. One whose teeth with age have grown long and triangular where they meet.

LONG REINS. Reins used for breaking in horses. The trainer walks behind the horse with the long reins attached to the bit, running via a roller or saddle to the trainer's hands.

In long reining, a horse learns to turn and back and also acquires a sensitive mouth. Long reining is a definite skill and people with rough hands should never be allowed to touch the long reins.

LOOSE BOX. A stable in which a horse is free to move about and can roll without being cast, with a stable door that he can look over.

LORIMER or **LORINER**. This is the name for the highly skilled craftsman who makes the bits and other metal parts of horse harness. The word comes from the old French *loremier* or Latin *lorum*.

This craft is centuries old and, before machinery as we know it today, enormous skill was required to make a bit for a horse's mouth which functioned correctly but which did not hurt the tender mouth.

Very ancient bits, in old British and Roman times, had to be made of the metals then available which were usually soft compared to today's steel and chromium. Imagine the skill necessary to make such a bit with just a hot fire and basic tools!

LOT OF HORSE. An expression used to describe a horse who is compact with good bone and who stands over plenty of ground.

LUNGING. To work a riderless horse on a single rein and

drive him in a circle. This is an elementary stage in breaking and an important one. Always make sure the horse turns the same number of times to right and left otherwise he can end up one-sided.

It is useful to lunge an over-fresh horse before the rider mounts. This saves embarrassment and rodeo performances!

MADE. A made horse is one who has been fully trained to all the aids and all aspects of stable management.

MAIDEN. A racer who has never won.

MAKE AND BREAK. A term used to denote the training of a young horse from his first handling until he is thoroughly conversant with all the aids.

This teaching takes place over many months and both skill and patience are required with kindness and firmness.

MAKE A NOISE. One whose wind is suspect because he makes a noise when being ridden.

MANÈGE. An indoor training school.

MANGER. Known to all. A good feeding manger should be kept clean and not be capable of being moved by the animal.

MARE. A female who has been used for breeding, though the name is used in conversation to describe any female horse over four years of age.

MARRIOTT'S BITLESS. A rather rare form of bitless bridle which is not as popular as the Hackamore.

MARTINGALE. An artificial aid. There are three types: Running, Standing and Irish.

The **Running** is composed of a neck strap with a portion running from it to the girth. The other end is of two pieces fastening on to each snaffle rein by rings through which go a rein apiece.

This martingale steadies a horse who is inclined to toss his head, and when used with a snaffle it gives firm control without being savage. It is also useful in protecting the horse's mouth when he is ridden by a learner who might accidentally job him.

The two top ends of the martingale should, when held loose, just reach the top of the withers. If long, they are useless and can be dangerous. Many a rider has come to grief with a too long martingale dangling over and getting hooked up on a gate.

There are variations of the Running martingale. One type has a web which, in effect, combines the Running and Irish martingales into one. In another the two ends clip onto the actual bit; this is very severe indeed.

The **Standing** martingale has one strap which fastens on to the noseband. This restrains a rearing horse or one who loves tossing his head and hitting his rider in the face. They are popular on the polo ground where sudden braking is necessary.

The **Irish** martingale is a favourite for racing. It consists of as short four-inch piece of leather, with two rings through which the reins are inserted. There is nothing round the horse's neck nor connecting to the girth. It is valuable again with horses who toss their heads and throw their reins about. It also keeps a horse very steady at the gallop.

A martingale with a neck strap can be useful to a rider who has loosened in the saddle. He can grab it and retain his balance without fear of jobbing the animal's mouth.

Never have too much slack hanging beneath the girth. It is not unknown for restless horses to catch a hind hoof and then there is utter panic.

82

Like everything you do with horses, use common sense. It is better than a world of book learning!

METHODY. An old-fashioned name for a horse with broken knees.

MEWS. Stables around an open square. Now highly esteemed as valuable homes for humans!

MEZAIR. A difficult Haute École movement in which the horse rears, holds its balance for a few seconds, drops down to the ground for a few paces then repeats the movement.

MILK TEETH. Foal's teeth, shed gradually when the permanent teeth arrive at the appropriate stage of development.

MISFIT. A poor horse of any breed or one who is used incorrectly, e.g. a jumper as a cart horse.

MISHANDLED. A horse who has been cruelly treated and knocked about.

MONDAY MORNING LEG. Puffy legs which can occur on Monday morning if the horse stands idle in his stable on the Sunday! Don't leave the animal there eating his head off. Take him for a walk at least. It will do you good after your Sunday's over-eating too!

MONGOLIAN HORSES. Mongolia is so far away many of you will not even know where it is but all will have heard of Genghis Khan! It is a country were the horse is next door to being worshipped. It is also the natural home of the only true wild horse, Prezewalski's or Mongolian Tarpan (*q.v.*).

Everyone rides and children often start before they can walk properly, while adults, minus a horse, do not feel properly 'dressed'.

Horses are kept in herds and are mostly dun or brown in colour although there are, of course, exceptions. When a herdsman wants to catch a horse he does not bother with a lariat like an American cowboy. He rides forth with a very long thin pole in one hand. Attached to the end of it is a loop and this is dropped over the head of the selected animal. Hey presto, the new mount is captured.

These horses look small to us, who are used to hunters up to seventeen hands, but they are tough, extremely rugged and enduring, capable of being used for many kilometres. The terrain is like the mounts, virgin, wild and includes all that Nature can throw at man or beast including rivers, streams, ravines and really wild country-side.

It is over this land that races are held. The greatest 'jockeys' are young children, girls and boys being equal,

and the race's distance depends upon the horse's age as well as that of its rider. Animals of 2 to 5 years will race about 10 kilometres and a little upwards although stallions are capable of going much further.

There are also adult races for which the enthusiasm is vociferous and highly active!

It is a great distance to travel to see these magnificent riders and their mounts. But Mongolia is a place to put on the 'I'd like to visit' agenda in case the lottery ticket comes up some day.

MONGOLIAN TARPAN or PREZEWALSKI'S HORSE. The world's only true wild horse. Others that run wild are all descended from domestic stock.

This animal is small and ugly with a head too large for his body. The colour is red-brown, dun or yellow with black points and sometimes a black stripe running down the spine. The muzzle is usually white.

For many years this was said to be an endangered species, and the late Gerald Durrell patiently collected a small herd in his zoo on Jersey. The Czech Republic also has a few of these animals, and they are known to breed in Mongolia. As that country is so far away, it is easier to view them in Jersey!

The antiquity of this horse cannot be disputed and by comparison it gives a very good idea of how far the modern type has progressed in height, weight and general looks since ancient times.

MORGAN. An American breed. A horse of great strength who is a fine riding animal. He is an excellent foundation animal for general breeding purposes.

MOUTHING SNAFFLE. A special type of snaffle from the centre piece of which dangle keys. This is used in breaking

85

when the object is to get the horse to slobber and develop a nice, wet mouth with sensitivity, as opposed to a hard, dry one. It is the dry-mouth horse who becomes the puller. The keys dangling from the bit encourage the horse to chomp on them and cause saliva to form.

MUD FEVER. This condition has other names which include Cracked or Greasy Heel and Rain Scald. Like many others it arises from two sources: a bacteria and the weather. There is nothing worse for a horse than to be constantly wet and caked with slimy mud that is left unattended. The body parts affected are the legs, belly, back and even the quarters. There will be swelling, redness, soreness and matted hair, under which will be found horrible and painful scabs. These latter can leak like an infected wound and you must get veterinarian attention.

It is better not to let this state of affairs arise in the first place. The animal's body must be kept dry and warm. If you come back from hard work the muddy parts should be hosed down then dried very thoroughly indeed. No half measures, please.

It is also useful to request your vet to prescribe a cream to be rubbed into the legs and belly before the horse is worked in bad conditions. Many vets make up their own cream specifically for this purpose.

With a severe case of Mud Fever it might become necessary to give the horse antibiotics but really only a bad and casual horse owner will let his animal get to this stage.

MULE. The offspring of a male ass and a female horse becomes a mule. They are usually sterile and incapable of breeding.

They are obstinate but are good workers if handled without too much bullying. They can stand up to sixteen hands and have long, small hooves and a tufted tail. They are very tough, less liable to disease than the horse and not so fussy about what they are given to eat. They can live longer than the horse.

MUSTANG. See BRONCO.

NAG. An old name for a small, cobby type horse.

NAGSMAN. Another old fashioned name for a man who schools and demonstrates a horse.

NAILS. It is most important to see that horse shoe nails are the correct length. The nail is made with one side flat from head to tip. When driven into the hoof the nail is inclined to veer sideways and so comes out of the foot at an angle. The nail is firmly hammered home. The protruding end is then twisted off and rasped flush with the hoof. The first nail is usually placed at the toe, then hammered in on alternate sides. See SHOEING.

NAPPY. A cunning, miserable horse given to sly bucking and biting when he thinks the rider or groom is unprepared. Definitely anti-social at all times and not worth bothering with!

NASAL GLEET. A form of Catarrh. Any discharge is a symptom of illness. Isolate the animal and if you suspect anything serious don't try to cure it yourself but get your veterinarian. In bad cases an injection of penicillin may be necessary. A steam head bath helps because, as with us, catarrh after a cold is most uncomfortable.

NATIONAL HUNT RACING. Racing over jumps. These may be solid as for steeplechasing or light hurdles which fall down if touched.

It is generally agreed that racing over jumps started about 1836 when hedges had grown after the Enclosures Act though it began even earlier in Ireland. In 1830 a race was held at Harlington Hill. The idea was to race the horses from one church steeple to another! The first proper steeplechase, as we know it, was held in 1836 at Liverpool and run twice round a two mile course. It was won by Captain Becher (pronounced Beecher), and everyone has heard of Becher's Brook on the Grand National Course. In 1838 the first National was run and won by Lottery. A Grand National Hunt Committee was formed in 1866 but this was disbanded in 1883 and reformed again in 1884. This is to steeplechasing what the Jockey Club is to Flat Racing. At one time the Jockey Club disdained their new brother, refusing to offer any aid or co-operation.

The greatest steeplechase in the world is the Grand National, run over 4½ miles of thirty tough fences.

NAVICULAR. A serious condition of the foot concerning the navicular bone and the surrounding area. There is still controversy regarding the cause. Most of the available treatment is aimed at removing pain but there is often a chronic state of inflammation in the affected foot. It usually applies to a front hoof because navicular of the rear is rare.

One should always suspect navicular if the horse rests a forefoot, which is unnatural, though acceptable with a hind foot. After work the lameness may go but the problem is still there.

Get the vet, who might suggest surgery. But the case might be hopeless and the horse, if a mare, could then be used only for breeding. With a gelding there would be a great problem if the animal had been bought for pure riding.

With a bad case there might only be one option, to put the animal down.

NEAR. Means left.

NECK REINING. To turn a horse without applying pressure on the bit, one drags the rein against the neck.

The right rein pressed against the neck means turn left and vice versa.

All well trained animals should respond to neck reining. The cowboy's horse is an artist at being neck-reined.

NEW FOREST. A British pony found in the New Forest, standing up to fourteen hands. They have varied colours though grey is rare. They are gay and alert with good tempers when broken but can often give trouble in the actual breaking process. They make ideal second ponies for children as well as being good fun to drive.

NEW ZEALAND RUG. A rug for the horse who lives in the open but who wants some protection against bad weather. It is made of heavy canvas and is just about waterproof. It fastens at the front, under the girth and at each hind leg with a strap that goes round the limb. They are ideal for clipped, weekend-only hunters who live out from Monday to Friday.

NIGGLE. A movement of the rider's hands when urging his horse to greater effort.

NOBBLING. A dangerous and illegal practice in which a drug of some kind is given to a horse to alter his behaviour and galloping ability. There are severe penalties at law. A doped horse can come down unexpectedly while galloping and be injured, while the unfortunate jockey might end up being trampled to death.

NORFOLK COB. An old fashioned cob that stood about fifteen hands and was used for both riding and driving.

NORTH FOREST. Soviet horses; rugged, hardy and of many varieties. Their use is for both riding and pulling especially the famous three-horse sleighs called troikas.

They have shaggy hair, thick manes and a layer of heavy fat against the extreme winter conditions. Their colours range from bay and roan to mouse and grey.

A few of the breeds are: Pechora, Mezen and Tavdas.

Because of the climate the animals tend to be small compared to British horses, but care and thought has been given to their breeding in the State Studs and they are useful animals.

NORWEGIAN. A small, tough breed of pony usually dun in colour with a tan muzzle and a black stripe on the back.

NOSEBAND. A part of the bridle which fits around the nose and on which the Standing martingale fastens. It should hang about two inches below the cheekbones and should allow two fingers width between it and the face. If kept highly polished it makes the whole bridle look most attractive. See also DROP NOSEBAND.

NOTIFIABLE DISEASES. Illnesses which, when they occur, must be notified to the authorities as they constitute a general danger to the health of all. They include Anthrax, Glanders, Epizootic Lymphangitis and Parasitic Mange. See ZOONOSES.

NUMNAH. Pads which fit beneath the saddle, made of thick felt or sheepskin. The only trouble with them is if they fit too closely they block the air from flowing down the back and cause considerable sweating. They must be kept very clean to minimise against sores, which is no easy task. Care must be taken to ensure that they do not work backwards under the saddle.

NUTS. Not the ones you sit and crack around the Christmas table. These nuts are manufactured horse food which combine proteins, carbohydrates and vitamins. The days of feeding simple, plain oats have long gone and nuts have usurped oats' place.

How much you feed depends on many factors: the animal's age and height, the amount and type of work he does and whether he lives in the stable or out in the field.

Do not hesitate to consult your family vet and read – carefully – the feeding instructions and formulae on the sack's side. Too much rich food is as bad for the horse as it is for man!

OATS. Oats are to horses what meat is to man. They are the high protein, muscle and energy food necessary for horses in hard work. They are the recognised equine grain and full of nutrition. But plain oats have generally given way to nuts.

Oats are fed whole, bruised or crushed. Bruised and crushed oats are easier to digest.

Horses in hard work need more oats than those doing gentle hacking and always remember that oats can go to a horse's head! A horse fed too many oats and receiving too little exercise will come out of his stable on his hindlegs just demanding that you fight him! Give the oats mixed with some good bran or other good quality food damp-ened slightly. Mix in some sliced carrots or apples if you like.

Oats are extremely heady to ponies so go very easy indeed; in fact, it is seldom necessary to give ponies oats at all.

Oats can be white or brown and they should smell sweet and wholesome with large grains and no mould anywhere. When broken they should show plenty of good colour content.

OESTRUS. The technical name for when the mare comes into season.

OFF. Meaning right.

ON THE BIT. Describes a horse who is going well into his bridle and who doesn't need any urging from his rider.

ON THE LEG. A description for a tall horse with long legs. Not complimentary!

OPIUM. This is the dried juice of the unripened poppy capsule and is used as a medication under strict veterinary control.

OVERBENT. This means the horse is bending his head too much at the poll and it is caused by a too severe bit or a heavy handed rider.

boots to suit.

OVER AT THE KNEE. Knees which are not quite straight but slightly bent. Horses are sometimes born like this although they can acquire them from overwork. It is often said that a horse with overbent knees is a very fast galloper as his legs can cover more ground in one stride. This, though, is a moot point.

OVERGROWN FOOT. A condition which arises when the animal's feet have been shod, the shoe not worn or removed and the hoof has grown too long. The hoof, like a fingernail, is constantly growing. When shod the hoof does not wear away normally as nature intended because it is not in direct contact with the ground.

Even if a horse does not wear his shoes out quickly it is always wise to have the farrier remove them periodically, pare the hoof then reshoe.

OVER REACH. This is caused when the hind feet swing too far forward and cut the front legs or heels. These cuts can be very painful. Bathe and treat with antiseptic and if necessary get special shoes fitted or make the animal wear

OVER THE STICKS. Popular term for racing over jumps.

PALOMINO. See ISABELLA. A very beautiful coloured horse. It was mentioned in Ancient History under the name of Xanthos. The skin colour is gold with a white or silver mane and tail.

It is a very popular horse in the United States and is becoming popular in Britain; there are many Palomino Societies. Although some people refer to this as a breed this is not yet accurate. The American Palominos have a reputation for gentleness combined with superior intelligence and beauty as well as making splendid riding animals.

PARALYSIS. A serious condition, as with man, whether it is caused by illness or accident. The limbs or body become incapable of action. This is a most complex subject on which only a veterinarian can be turned to for help.

PARASITES. Another subject requiring a tome of its own! All parasites live on a host whether it be human, animal or insect. All are totally unwelcome.

Some obvious parasites are worms and warbles under the skin. Any small lump under the skin in summer is probably a warble grub ready to hatch itself. Large worms can be seen in the droppings. Where parasites are concerned you simply must get professional assistance immediately.

PARASITIC MANGE. A virulent, notifiable disease transmutable to man. This first shows itself when the animal's hair begins to drop out, then the papules form and the horse is in great pain from itching. You must, by law, get professional help.

PARDUBICE. This is a very famous steeplechase race run by the Czech Republic usually in the early Autumn. It certainly rivals our Grand National and is a little longer in length. It is a tough course and not all on grass; part is run on harrowed earth which, with rain, can make heavy going.

The most notorious fence is the Taxisus which rivals Becher's Brook on our Grand National Course at Aintree.

As Red Rum was the darling of the British public and forever remembered and connected with the Grand National, so do the Czechs have similar reverence for their wonder horse called Zeleznik. He won the race three times. He was a splendid jumper with a great turn of speed although, to look at, there was nothing startling about him.

A few British chasers and jockeys ride in the Pardubice and although places have been obtained, we have not, yet, had a winner over this ferocious course.

PARTURITION. This is the act of giving birth to the young. A normal healthy mare and foal will need no assistance. The foal should be born with its nose resting on the extended forelegs and it should quickly get to its feet and instinctively suckle. Where complications are suspected you will, long before this stage, have arranged for the veterinarian to be present.

Animals make no fuss over birth. Leave them alone but watch from a distance just in case help is required

PASSAGE. An advanced movement performed to right or left when the horse crosses his legs. All well schooled horses should be able to passage. The object of teaching this is to obtain better balance, to make the animal supple and to strengthen his back muscles.

The movement is performed at right angles. In the half pass, though, the animal moves forwards and to one side.

The rider uses legs and hands. He lays the reins on the neck, checks any forward movement with the bit and drives with one leg. To go to the left, check with the bit, lay the reins against the right side of the neck, squeeze with the right leg while the left restrains behind the girth.

These passaging movements are tiring to a young horse so do not overdo this schooling. Little and often is better than a long, exhausting lesson which might become boring.

PASTERN. That part of the leg between the fetlock joint and the hoof.

PATELLA. The name for the bone which lies at the front of the stifle joint and equals man's knee. When dislocated it is known as a slipped stifle.

PEACOCKY. A flashy horse who looks good but which upon closer examination is not what it appears. In other words, a con horse.

PEAT. See BEDDING.

PEGASUS. The winged horse of ancient legend.

PELHAM. A type of combination bit ridden with double reins. The bar may be metal or hard, compressed rubber.

PERCHERON. A heavy draught horse native to France. The colour is grey. Percherons stand between sixteen and seventeen hands and are very distinguished in that they lack the heavy thick feather found on other large draught horses. They are believed to be descended from post horses. Napoleon had two chargers named Godolphin and Gallipoli. These two great animals gave the breed its present day stamp of type and colour. Even though so large and heavy they are active. With their large eyes and splendid crests they have a regal bearing.

PIAFFE. An Haute École movement when the horse marks time on one spot with the dismounted rider standing alongside.

PIEBALD. Classed as an odd colour, this horse has large black patches on a white background.

PINTO. An American name for a piebald or skewbald colour.

PIPE OPENER. A short, brisk gallop to open a horse's pipes before more extensive exercise or work like an actual race.

PLAITING. A horse's mane is plaited to improve its appearance. Six or seven plaits are made on the neck with one plait between the eyes. The hair is divided evenly and a plait made. This is sewn at the end then the whole is doubled up again into a small ball and sewn firmly. Use thread and do sew tightly. Nothing looks more untidy than a plait coming undone!

PLATE. A very special light shoe worn by racers for the race only.

PLATER. A race horse who has sunk to the level of only running in cheap races or unimportant races. In such races the winner and second are usually sold automatically.

PNEUMONIA. As serious as the human variety which can cripple the lungs and cause death. This requires skilled treatment and drugs. There is a high temperature, rapid breathing, a racing pulse, sweating and then shivering fits. Once the horse lies down you know the situation is critical. The horse must be kept warm and, at the same time, have fresh air without draughts.

POINTS OF THE HORSE. The main points are shown in the accompanying illustration.

POINT TO POINT. A race run over natural jumps and under National Hunt Rules but only for Amateur riders and horses who have been 'regularly and fairly hunted'.

Many famous Grand National horses started their career

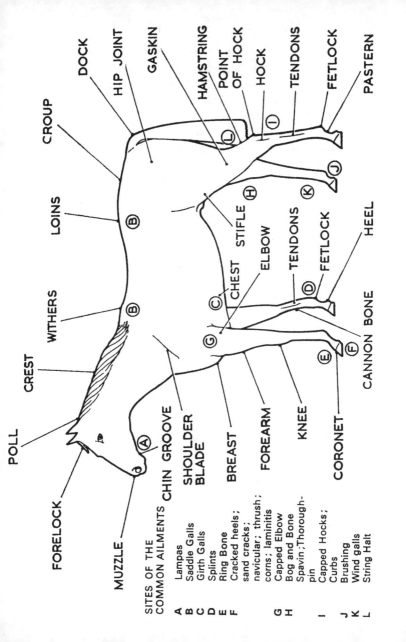

POLL

CREST

FORELOCK

WITHERS

LOINS

CROUP

DOCK

HIP JOINT

GASKIN

HAMSTRING

POINT OF HOCK

HOCK

TENDONS

FETLOCK

PASTERN

MUZZLE

CHIN GROOVE

SHOULDER BLADE

BREAST

FOREARM

KNEE

CORONET

CANNON BONE

FETLOCK

TENDONS

HEEL

FETLOCK

ELBOW

CHEST

STIFLE

SITES OF THE
COMMON AILMENTS

A   Lampas
B   Saddle Galls
C   Girth Galls
D   Splints
E   Ring Bone
F   Cracked heels;
    sand cracks;
    navicular; thrush;
    corns; laminitis
G   Capped Elbow
H   Bog and Bone
    Spavin;Thorough-
    pin
I   Capped Hocks;
    Curbs
J   Brushing
K   Wind galls
L   String Halt

Point to Pointing. The name originated from the early days when the race was from 'one point to another'.

POISONOUS PLANTS. The most well known is the wicked **ragwort** plant (*q.v.*) because, although this has a bitter taste, enabling some horses to avoid it, there are others who lack all sense and feeling.

Hemlock must be added to this list with the **buttercup**, the **acorn** and all forms of **ivy**. Another wicked plant is the **yew** tree (*q.v.*). Fortunately most yew trees appear to grow in church yards and it is not likely you will turn your horse out there. If, though, he goes into a field which abuts a church yard with an overhanging yew, you have a problem.

The best way to deal with this is to have a tactful word with the Vicar and explain the situation, in great detail if he is not a horsey man, and ask his permission to cut back the overhanging branches. Strictly speaking, in the law of Torts, you do not have to ask. You can lop off the offending branches just as long as you return them to their rightful owner. But it is better to get permission because even vicars have been known to throw a tizzy now and again!

POISONS. Another vast subject best left to the professional man! If the horse is suspected of having taken poison, rush for him.

POKING THE NOSE. An irritating gesture when the horse pokes his nose into the air and, consequently, does not look where he is going or respond to the bit. Correct instantly with the legs and a Standing martingale.

POLICE HORSE. A fully trained police horse, usually a half breed, is a model of good behaviour in the face of man's stupidity. It will ignore shouts, shots, traffic, waving objects and noisy crowds, all of which require an animal

POISONOUS PLANTS: *Top left to right*: Ragwort, Yew.
Middle: Buttercup, Hemlock. *Foot*: Ivy, Acorn

with a special temperament and hours of patient training.

Police horses must also be sure footed as they work on road surfaces liable to have oil on them. British Police Horses are usually ridden in an Army Reversible bit with Army Saddles. A baton is fixed to one side of the saddle and there are large D rings for attaching any other useful object.

They must be fully trained in the aids and ridden one handed.

POLL. The tender spot between the horse's ears. Never tap a horse there. They hate it. At that point the skull is thin like a man's at the temple.

POLO PONY. An animal bred for the game. They are under fifteen hands and must be capable of sudden stops and rapid turns, being able to reverse and spin 'on a sixpence'. Most good Polo Ponies have some Arab blood in their breeding although they are not a breed in themselves. They are highly trained in the aids and must have great stamina.

POMMEL. The rising arch at the front of the saddle.

PONY. An animal under fifteen hands found in a variety of breeds in Britain. They are ideal for children and nervous or elderly adults. The British breeds are Dartmoor, Exmoor, Fell and Dale, New Forest, Shetland, Welsh and Highland.

PONY CLUB. A first class organisation for children and teenagers which teaches, runs camps and holidays, and organises competitions. Each Hunt has its own branch.

POP. A horse is said to have a good pop when it is a big jumper with a fine spring.

POSTING. To rise from the saddle (by standing up and down in the stirrups) at the trot in tune to the horse's action.

Many American and Australian riders do not do this. Neither do the military.

POTATOES. This common tuber can be poisonous to the horse if old or rotten. He will get staggers which, as the name implies, makes him stagger in a weakened condition, suffering from an inability to drink despite a great thirst. There is heavy breathing, a fast pulse and general signs of distress. Get help, though the moral is: examine the potatoes first!

PREGNANCY. The term of the mare's gestation period is eleven months. As with all females the most obvious sign is a swollen body but earlier signs can sometimes be noted. Turn the mare to the right and movement might be seen. Needless to say, only the veterinary performs an internal examination and then only if necessary.

The mare should not be molly-coddled but neither should she be worked too hard or to long. When she is big she should rest entirely. Stop the use of the wisp and groom with care and gentleness. Let the mare have plenty of fresh air and walking. Let her out during the day. She must have a sensible diet with lucerne being a good feed as it is rich in salts. As she gets near her time observe her carefully but let her manage by herself if everything is normal. Often the mare's teats wax over exactly two days before she gives birth, which is a useful pointer.

PREZEWALSKI'S HORSE. See MONGOLIAN TARPAN.

PULSE. The pulse rate varies depending upon age, health and sex but the average can be taken as being between 35-45 beats per minute. The easiest place to take this is between the angle of the jaw and the region of the lower incisor teeth or the inside of the forearm near the elbow joint.

QUALIFICATIONS. When the writer started work with horses all that was required was an ability to ride and a little nous. A kind of long apprenticeship was served and the keen groom made sure of moving from one type of stable to another to broaden experience.

Nowadays, we live in an age of bits of paper. This is not to deride paper qualifications though, in the writer's very hard-acquired knowledge, a wealth of practical experience can offset bits of paper.

The British Horse Society, the BHS, and the Association of British Riding Schools, the ABRS, are the organisations to which the student should apply. For the BHS lessons and examinations, membership of the Society is vital. The age at which studies can commence with the BHS is 16 years, 17 years for the 3rd stage and 20 years for the 4th stage examinations.

The minimum age for the ABRS studies is 16 years for levels 1 and 2. But the student must be 18 years or over to sit for the Diploma and the student must have had two years' practical experience.

There are also courses of study, with appropriate qualifications, for the Horse Care and Management qualifications and the Racehorse Care at levels 2 and 3.

Some of these courses are not cheap so the student should ask around for general information, decide which type of horse work appeals most and only then make a positive decision. The BHS is a mine of information and practical help so do not hesitate to contact them. Good luck with whatever you decide to do! Horses can be very aggravating animals at times but, they probably have a similar opinion about us humans! See also EMPLOYMENT.

QUARTER HORSE. A small horse bred specially in the

USA to turn cattle and rope them. They are as clever as trial-breed sheep dogs. They know exactly when to turn, swerve, stop and baulk the cattle in every move. They are also used in races of a quarter of a mile. They are now imported into Britain; they are a specific breed.

QUESTION. A rider puts the question to his horse when he asks him to go faster or tackle a stiff jump. He puts him to the test.

QUIDDOR. One who chews his food then sprinkles it on the ground. Quidding is also known as cudding.

The cause is often bad teeth or a mouth injury. Get the veterinarian.

QUIET. A word used to describe a horse for sale but one on which legal actions have taken place!

What is quiet to one person may be sluggish to another! If the horse is supposed to be quiet in traffic does that include for instance heavy, moving concrete mixers? – Strictly speaking a quiet horse is one who does not kick, bite, rear or have any other funny antics for the unwary.

QUITTOR. A leg injury connected with the cartilages caused by blows. There is lameness and with an open wound even a discharge. Get help.

A **quitter** is a horse who gives up too easily.

RACE HORSE. A Thoroughbred often of great value and the most expensive animal to own. Indeed, many animals are so valuable they can only be owned by syndicates.

RACING. See FLAT & NATIONAL HUNT RACING.

RACK UP. To chain a horse to his manger while the stable is cleaned or the animal groomed.

RADIAL PARALYSIS. Also known as Dropped Elbow and a serious condition arising from accident or other injury. The limb cannot take the body's weight nor can it be moved. Get professional assistance at once.

RAGWORT. A wildflower with many yellow or slightly orange petals and a red stem. When the leaves are crushed, it has a peculiar odour. The Latin name of the most common variety is *Senecio Jacobaea*. There are also the Hoary Ragwort, Marsh Ragwort, Broad Leaved Ragwort and others.

It is poison to the horse, whether growing fresh or dried, when it might be mixed in with hay. When fresh, some horses might not be badly affected while others would succumb. These plants contain a substance called Pyrroliszidene Alkaloid which affect the liver. Death can occur with five to ten days.

Before turning your horse into a field do check whether ragwort grows there. It is also prudent to check with your Forage Merchant as to where his hay was grown.

To destroy this noxious weed the root must be dug up and burnt thoroughly. A constant watch must be kept because of windborne seeds. Under the 1959 Weeds Act the landowner has a duty to eradicate the plant.

RAIN SCALD. This is an old fashioned name for an infection which a horse can get when it is subjected to prolonged cold soaking. Lesions will appear on the withers, back and quarters and the Vet must be consulted. Anyone who looks after the horse properly, though, will not have to contend with this condition. If a horse does suffer from Rain Scald, from downright neglect, there is a distinct possibility the owner might find himself liable for prosecution by the RSPCA.

READY. To prepare a horse for a race or show.

REARER. A horse who stands on his hind legs and rears right up, reaching for the sky. Never hang on to the reins;

Ragwort *Senecio Jacobaea*

you can pull the horse over on top of yourself. Lean forward, tap the poll and sit still. This is easier said than done!

Discourage this vice with a Standing martingale. One very old and drastic method of curing a rearer was to allow him to rear his protest without a rider on his back and pull the horse over backwards with long reins. This is not to be recommended as the animal can break his back.

Keep a rearer's head down and ride with your own hands low.

REIN BACK. Press with the calf muscles, feel on the reins and the trained horse will back in a straight line. This is a valuable exercise for the opening of gates. With a young horse it helps to have an assistant who presses the horse's nose as the rider gives the aids. The horse soon learns what is expected.

REINS. The best reins from the bit to the hands are made of plaited nylon. Quite unbreakable but do keep them clean and soft for the sake of your own hands if the horse pulls!

RESTRAINT. A method used to make a horse obey with the aid of the voice, bridle or twitch (*q.v.*).

RIDING STYLES. These are varied the world over. The jockey rides with short leathers and his bottom in the air to get all the weight off the horse's back.

The Australian stockman and the American cowboy ride long with a straight leg and deep seat which they have found most suitable for spending days in the saddle.

The huntsman rides fairly long but with a definite bend at the knee for jumping.

A really good rider is capable of adopting all styles to suit the animal or situation as it comes to hand.

RIG. An imperfectly castrated male horse.

RING BONE. This appears on the pastern and causes lameness. The actual cause is still open to debate though continual foot concussion on hard surfaces does not help.

The lameness is often slow at the start without even heat or swelling but gradually the enlargement is seen and only a veterinarian can treat it.

RINGWORM. Also known as Favus or even Herpes. It is an unpleasant skin condition caused by spores or fungi. These live either on the skin's surface or in the hairs of the region affected.

To the eye, it may show as a dry and raised crusty skin from which the hairs have vanished. The skin itself might be red and inflamed and perhaps oozing a nasty fluid.

Isolate the horse and get your vet quickly. Practise strict hygiene for other animals and yourself: it is infectious, and can be passed on to man.

ROACH BACK. Also known as Hog Back. A conformation fault where the horse's back curves upwards.

ROADSTER. An old fashioned name for a saddle horse.

ROAN. A coat which is a mixture of colours. A Red Roan has a coat with red coloured hairs sometimes sprinkled with white while the Blue, as the colour implies, is also mixed with white. A Red Roan has a chestnut mane and tail; a Blue, black points, mane and tail. Roans are not common.

ROGUES BADGE. Another name for blinkers attached to the hood because they are only worn by troublesome horses to make them run straight or concentrate on the job in hand. The word rogue also means an awkward or bad-tempered animal.

ROLLER. Also known as a Surcingle. This strap goes

around the animal's body to hold the clothing in place. The best type has a metal arch at the withers to minimise a sore back when the horse rolls.

ROPE BROKEN. An American term for a horse who has been educated to the use of the lasso, who will stand and take the strain when the rope is connected from the saddle to a struggling steer without the rider's help.

ROUGHING. This means the farrier will remove the shoes and turn down a length of calkin. It helps prevent slipping during bad weather.

ROUGH OFF. A horse is roughed off when work is finished for the season. Slowly, high-protein diet is cut down; dirt is allowed to accumulate in his coat and his clothing is gradually reduced and finally removed. He is turned into the field for an hour each day, and then two, then all day and finally at night as well.

The shoes have been removed and the animal is given his freedom to enjoy his holiday.

ROUGH UN. A horse who bucks, kicks, rears and fights for the sheer hell of it. An equine delinquent not worth the trouble of fighting.

ROYAL HANOVERIAN CREAM. A very beautiful cream horse not unlike a Lipizanner with strength and character. They were originally bred in Hanover and were very popular with Queen Victoria as carriage horses on State occasions.

RUBBER PADS. Pads made to place below the shoe to cushion against jarring. Then nails hold them in position.

RUG. An article of clothing which goes on top of the blanket and is made of canvas for night wear and smartly coloured for daytime.

RUGBY PELHAM. A type of pelham bit not seen often.

The main difference is that the top reins fit on to a detached ring as opposed to the ordinary pelham which is one solid curb bit. Used with double reins.

RUNNING LOOSE. A race horse whose stable has elected not to place bets on it – for reasons best known to themselves!

RUNNING OUT. Horses turned out to grass to rest, hunters roughed off. The name also refers to the horse that runs out, i.e. away from a fence. Collect the animal, keep him firm and straight and drive him with the legs. Break him of his habit. With a steeplechase horse it can cause a disaster, as happened at Foinavon's Grand National when many well placed horses were recklessly brought down by running out.

SADDLE. There are many varieties of saddle all over the world, some beautiful, costly affairs, others crude and uncomfortable. The British saddles are:

> The light weight racing saddle
> The forward cut jumping saddle
> The standard hunting saddle
> The military saddle
> The Dressage saddle
> The side saddle (*q.v.*)

The **racing saddle** is feather light so that the jockey can make the necessary weight. It is often a mere pad on the back with tiny stirrups and light girth.

The **jumping saddle** has the flaps cut very forward so that the show jumper's knees can slide onto the shoulders of his horse as he gets his weight really forward.

The **hunting saddle** is designed for many hours riding

and general use, whilst the **military** and **police** saddles have a higher cantle with a back part behind for fastening objects.

The **Australian stockman's saddle** is a dream of comfort with its deep seat, high pommel and cantle plus large knee rolls. The **American cowboys's saddle** has a horn at the pommel onto which can be fastened his rope with another high and comfortable cantle.

Australian stirrups are usually placed so that the leather buckle is just above the iron and not under the saddle bars as with a British saddle.

The American western stirrup is sometimes made of wood, thick and solid.

The most important part of the saddle is the tree which is the spine of the saddle. It is most important with high-withered horses that the saddle arch clears the back, otherwise dreadful and painful sores occur. The tree is made of iron or any other strong substance and the rest of the saddle is built around the tree.

Saddles should be kept clean and well soaped. Great attention should be paid to the part underneath which fits on the animal's back.

SADDLE GALLS. These nasty sores are caused by ill-fitting saddles. If left untreated they can turn to foul-smelling ulcers. To ride a horse with a galled back is downright cruelty.

If galls develop find the cause, then while curing the gall have the saddle put right.

Bathe the galls, get them really clean, then dust with antiseptic powder and let the fresh air and sun do the rest. If necessary exercise the horse on the lunging rein.

SALT. Every living creature requires salt. Fasten a salt lick

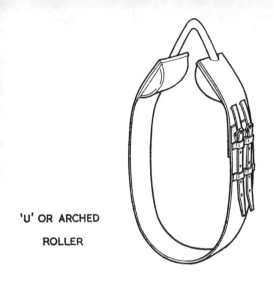

'U' OR ARCHED
ROLLER

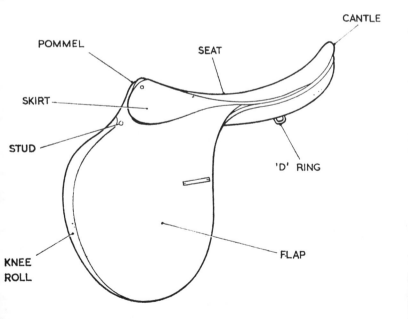

POMMEL

SEAT

CANTLE

SKIRT

STUD

'D' RING

KNEE
ROLL

FLAP

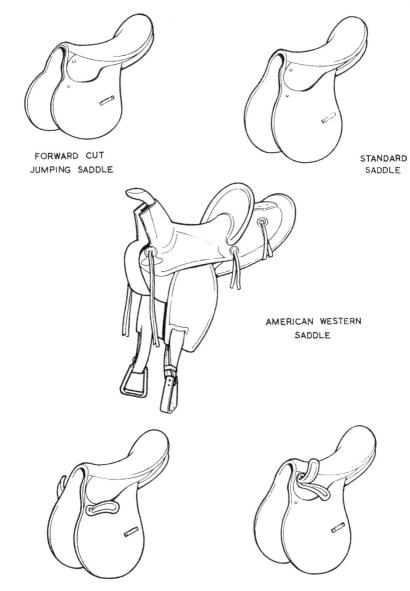

FORWARD CUT
JUMPING SADDLE

STANDARD
SADDLE

AMERICAN WESTERN
SADDLE

AUSTRALIAN BUCK-JUMPING SADDLE

LADIES SIDE SADDLE

on the stable wall so that your horse can take a lick as and when he fancies.

SAND. See BEDDING.

SAND CRACK. A vertical crack in the hoof. The farrier must remove the shoe and then you must get the veterinary. Sometimes the crack is deep and long with heat and pus present. Clean most thoroughly.

One way to close the crack is to drive a nail across it, clench the ends off and leave it in place for a while.

SANITATION. Stables must have good drainage and always smell sweet and clean. Do not be miserly with the disinfectant!

SAWDUST. See BEDDING.

SCHOOLING. The horse's education when he learns manners, the aids and how to behave in general. Patience is required. Make the lessons small but often. Constant repetition is the secret to successful schooling.

SCOURING. Looseness of the bowels, also known as Diarrhoea. This can be a symptom of many illnesses, so get help.

SCOWLING. When a horse is annoyed he shows it. He flattens his ears, rolls his eyes and puts a scowl on his face. Watch out! Because if he really means business both heels and teeth will be brought into play!

SCREW. A poor weedy horse.

SEASON. In season, common term for Oestrus (*q.v.*).

SEAT. A rider's position in the saddle. A good seat is strong, firm, graceful and comfortable. A good way to acquire a proper seat is to do plenty of bare back riding or to ride without stirrups.

SEEDY TOE. A condition affecting the horse's hoof at the toe when the foot becomes dry and crumbling in appearance. Bad shoeing is often the cause. Skilled help is necessary because if left untreated the condition spreads, causing bad lameness.

SELLING RACE. After this type of race the winner is always sold.

SEMINOLE. The type of horse that belonged to the American Indian tribe of that name. Semonoles were small but full of life and fire and great favourites with the warriors.

SET FAIR. To clean out the animal's stable, groom him, put down fresh bedding, water and hay and to leave the animal clean, tidy and comfortable.

SHAFTS. The parts of the vehicle that link it to the horse pulling it. The shafts fit on either side of the horse and are attached to him by the traces and other parts of his harness.

SHELL FEET. Thin soled feet which are brittle and unhealthy. A farrier's nightmare.

SHETLAND PONY. A British pony from the Islands of the north. They are smallest of the pony breeds and are sometimes called Shelties. They are measured in inches and not hands. The smallest recorded was only 26 inches and the average is 40 inches.

They have heads with bold, clever eyes, wide nostrils, thick manes and tails and lovely compact bodies. All colours can be found. They are incredibly tough and hardy. They are a very pure breed and a great favourite with us all.

SHIRE. The world's largest draught horse and British. They have fantastic strength and a good stallion will stand at seventeen hands and pull a ton.

They are most colours, though dark brown is favoured. They have thick, flowing feather, sweeping manes and

114

tails. Their appearance is regal.

SHOEING. Shoes are placed upon hooves to protect them from excessive wear on hard surfaces, especially roads. Even the Romans protected their mounts' feet with crude shoes made from leather and straw.

The modern shoe is made from a thin bar of iron which the farrier heats and moulds into the shape of the horse's foot. He hammers and beats the red hot metal for a first fitting. Before this, he pares the foot, trimming it smooth, works the shoe then places it, very hot, upon the hoof to ascertain the fit. If unsatisfactory the farrier reheats the shoe again in his roaring forge and hammers away once more. There is constant fitting and hammering until the shoe fits that particular hoof perfectly.

Front shoes have a central turned up clip at the toe which helps to keep the shoe in position. Hind shoes have two clips which are always set at the side, i.e. right and left and never in the centre, because this might hurt the tendons of the front leg if the horse's stride suddenly became extra large. There are usually four nails on the outside of the shoe and three on the inside, which again avoids unnecessary bruises and cuts from a stumble.

Riding horses have shoes made with an extra grip provided by a ridge grove and these are called fullered shoes. Horses which pull carts have shoes with a plain, flat surface but extra high calkins at the rear for gripping.

A farrier's tools are a claw hammer, heavy rasp, paring knife and considerable human muscle. He also has a pair of strong pincers for removing shoes.

A feather edged shoe is one which is lighter on one side than the other. These would be placed on the feet of horses who, when lying down, cut themselves.

Three quarter shoes are fitted on horses with capped hocks or elbows. A roller is for the careless horse who drags his toes, stumbles and threatens to come down. Mere iron tips may be worn by horses out at grass if they have soft feet.

Never forget the saying 'No foot – no hoss'!

There are times when shoes loosen. The nails, called clenches, work loose. When this happens get your farrier to call. Sometimes he might simply tighten the nails with a few hefty hammer blows. Or, on the other hand, he might remove and refasten it completely. Don't tell him what to do about hooves! He is the expert after a most arduous training; let him take the decisions!

SHORT. A horse goes short when he is lame.

Get help for this. With bridle or halter, run with the horse away from your assistant then run back to him with the horse trotting alongside. The short horse will show because the horse will nod his head as the painful foot hits the ground or those particular tendons stretch. This means you must run him with his head held loosely. This is an impossible test to try alone.

Never forget the horse is a pretty stoical animal. He won't bawl and shriek or cry when in pain *but* he will try to show you with body language, i.e. by nodding when you trot with him when that hurt leg or foot has to be placed on the ground.

SHOULDER. The large bone in front of the saddle. All good riding animals must have a wide, sloping shoulder. The cart animal should have a straight one so that the collar fits easily.

The main shoulder injury is dislocation from a fall and this is most serious and requires professional attention.

116

SHY FEEDER. A horse who does not clean up his feed or who is easily distracted and must be tempted to eat. Never out-face this type of animal with too large meals. Little and often is the answer.

SHYING. A perfectly natural reflex move which horses make when frightened. They turn aside abruptly. The rider must soothe his horse and insist he goes back to the object, even if this takes all day and night. The whip is rarely useful unless the horse is shying from cussedness; then a couple of sharp raps should knock some sense back into his head.

SIDE BONE. Strictly speaking these are cartilage and not bone conditions. They should be taken seriously and the veterinarian called. They can be felt as a small swelling which appears above the coronet, i.e. where the hoof ends and the leg starts.

While forming, there may be lameness but once they have formed they are often present without pain. Road concussion is a prime cause although heredity can come into it also. They may cause complications later in life which is why help, at the offset, is sensible.

SIDE SADDLE. The lady's saddle which allows her to ride with both legs on the same side, the left. Two horns project from the saddle and the legs wrap around these horns although the lady still sits in the centre. All side saddles must have a tight balance girth. This is of critical importance.

Do make sure the saddle fits properly because galls can form.

A lady riding side saddle looks most elegant, but over jumps these saddles can be extremely dangerous. If the horse comes down the lady is not thrown clear. The horns trap her legs and many a broken pelvis has followed such a fall.

The lady wears breeches and boots covered overall by a habit or long flowing skirt, black in colour. There is one stirrup and it is vitally important that this is the exact length. It is this solitary stirrup which keeps the leg jammed under the bottom horn.

SKEWBALD. An odd colouring, black excepted, composed of large coloured patches upon a white background.

SLEEP. The horse is a light sleeper, which explains why few owners are able to sneak up on their animals and catch them having a doze! The animal sleeps with its eyes semi-open, lying flat on its side and for short periods only. Horses do not need as much sleep as humans. They have an uncanny ability of being able to sleep standing. The horse can do this because of his peculiar body structure by which the body weight is taken by tendons and ligaments and not the muscles. The joints also can be 'locked' into a position! While the animal is, like us, unconscious when asleep, because of his highly developed reflex system the muscles are strong and prepared for instant flight or a doubled-barrelled kick!

SLING. A device which supports a horse by taking his weight off the ground with a block and tackle. Used for certain wounds and fractures or for transporting a horse aboard a ship. They must be fitted with care.

SNAFFLE. An ancient bit used to raise a horse's head, still used extensively. It is a good all-purpose bit for general riding with either a straight unbroken bar or a twisted broken middle piece fastened with a simple joint.

The most popular bit for race horses.

SNIP. A small white mark on the forehead or an odd white mark on the legs or body. It also means a horse brought at a bargain price.

SOCK. White markings on one or more legs which come up to the fetlock joints. Above this they are called stockings.

SORE BACK. Caused by badly fitted saddles or learners rolling around off balance. They are as painful to the horse as a blister is to us and the treatment is the same. Clean, dust with antiseptic powder and keep pressure away until healed.

SORE SHINS. Soreness of the shins is brought on by concussion from hard riding on solid ground or too much fast work on hard roads. Rest the legs and don't ride the horse to death on the roads.

SORRELL. The American name for chestnut.

SOUND. The description for an animal who has nothing at all wrong with him, i.e. sound in wind, limb and eyes.

SOUP PLATE FEET. Enormous feet, so large they are out of proportion to the body.

SPANISH RIDING SCHOOL OF VIENNA. This famous school is part of Austria's history. The classical art of horsemanship and riding has been perpetuated for over 400 years the very noble Lipizzaner horses. Their federal stud is based at Piber.

Vienna is the only place worldwide where this classical riding in its most pure form, known as Haute École, is held to its excellence, having come down to us from 1572. Its fantastic classical jumps are known as the Schools or Airs above the Ground.

The Lipizzaner is the oldest pure bred horse in Europe and its stud rules are very strict. These horses' ancestors came from Berbers, brought into Spain about 800 AD. The foal is usually born dark but, as the animal grows, it turns into that beautiful grey which the unhorsey call white. It is the stallions who are trained, over a long period of time and with incredible patience, to perform the Haute École movements with or without a rider. Only a very few talented stallions are capable of undergoing this long education.

Some of the movements are:

the **Pesade,** in which the horse raises his forelegs with a body balanced at a 45° angle

the **Levade**, a little bit like this but with the entire weight moving to the hindquarters with bent haunches

the **Courbette**, which starts with the Levade. Then the stallion jumps forward a number of paces, with its forelegs always bent and off the ground

the **Capriole**, in which the horse leaps from the ground with all four legs simultaneously then, with its body horizontal, kicks violently with the hind legs.

At regular intervals this incredible School comes to Britain to give shows, to music, mounted and unmounted, at Wembley or the NEC, Birmingham. Worth every penny of the entry money to watch. Do try to go.

SPAVINS. A condition of the hock divided into Bog or Bone Spavins. **Bog** is a puffy swelling on the inside and upper part of the hock joint caused by sprain or overwork. Pain may be present and cold applications should be applied. Sometimes a strong embrocation helps. Give gentle walking exercise.

Bone Spavin is a serious disease of the hock bones. A hard enlargement is found on the inner and lower part of the joint. Again this can also be caused by sprain, overwork or bad shoeing. Get the veterinarian in for this one, without hesitation.

SPEEDY CUTTING. This is caused by bad action where the hindlegs cut the forelegs. Alter the hind shoes. A horse with this continual fault is unsafe to ride at speed.

SPLINTS. These are bony enlargements on the side of the cannon bone of the front legs mostly found on young animals. They are rare on the hind legs and after six years of age. While forming they cause pain and lameness but once hard they do not often give trouble. Concussion will bring them on or overwork, as well as vitamin deficiencies in foals.

However, a splint which forms under the knee should be viewed very seriously because of the action of that joint. One lower down on the cannon bone is usually only a nuisance while it is forming. Many cases of splint lameness are helped by cold-water hosing and rest. If the lameness persists, though, the veterinary will fire and break the splint up with either pin or bar firing. This is classed as an operation.

SPRAINED TENDONS. Although the horse might not be lame at the walk he will be when trotted. Thickening, heat, inflammation and swelling will be present and the only real answer will be rest and plenty of it. A cream can be obtained from the vet, spread on cotton wool and placed over the area. It is then held in place with bandages. Sometimes if the sprain is a very bad one, the tendons might remain thick for ever, with a constant doubt about the horse's soundness for hard work.

SPRAINS. These are injuries of the joints from a slip or tumble. They can hurt and only time, rest and cold water will do any good. A back sprain requires professional help.

SPURS. An artificial aid and one of the best – when worn by the good rider. They cannot be seen or anticipated by the horse and come in many shapes, sizes and degrees of downright cruelty. The usual British ones are blunt with an angled elbow.

STABLE or BOX. The horse's home. It should be roomy, warm, dry and free from draughts, and with plenty of fresh air as well as an interesting view for the horse to study! It keeps him out of mischief, like crib biting!

There should be a top and a bottom door, the top door being shorter. There should be a good central drainage channel which connects with outside mains drains. A sound manger, running water which the horse learns to operate himself, electric power with the point suitably shielded against mischievous teeth and no rough or sharp projections. It is most important that the stable is large enough to allow the horse to get down and roll without casting himself. The best stables face the sun. A horse loves standing with his head over the door, nodding in the sun but constantly aware of everything going on.

STALE. To urinate. A horse should always be encouraged to stale after work and before he eats or drinks, to avoid colic. The rustle of straw with a soft whistle will encourage him.

STALL. An old-fashioned living place for the horse where he was tied up all the time.

STALLION. An adult male horse used for breeding.

STANDING MARTINGALE. See MARTINGALES.

STAR. A patch of white hair on the forehead bigger than a snip.

STAR GAZER. A horse who carries his head too high and doesn't look where he is going! A positive menace. Tie his head down with a Standing martingale.

STAYER. A horse with guts who never gives up.

STEAMING. This is excellent for horses with colds or other illnesses where breathing is laboured.

Fill a bucket with good dry hay, place in a large sack, pour 2 gallons of boiling water over this and any drugs which you may have been prescribed, then hold the end of the sack pinched together tightly around the horse's nose and mouth.

The treatment should continue for about ten minutes. It is wise to have an assistant because rising steam can frighten the animal.

STEEPLE CHASE. See NATIONAL HUNT RACING & POINT TO POINT.

STICKY. A horse who messes about and, when jumping his fences, dithers to right or left, changes his mind and decides to jump after all, or not.

STIRRUP. Also known as the iron. The rider's foot rests in it. After the invention of the wheel, it was the next most important discovery of early man. All transport was on horseback in early days but before the stirrup even the strongest man did not have a secure seat.

When warriors charged at each other many were promptly thrown. Then the stirrup was invented and the art of riding and warfare changed! The warrior now had a firmer seat in battle. He could ride longer distances without tiring and was more in tune with his mount.

Stirrups are made of metal or wood. In Britain they are always metal. It is important that the stirrup is the correct fit. If too large the foot can slip through and, if thrown, the rider is dragged with the risk of most serious injury. The same applies with a stirrup too small.

A good stirrup is one which bends away at the top, so stopping the rider's ankle joint being rubbed. This is called a cramped stirrup.

With children, always remember their feet are continually growing and getting larger.

STOCKHOLM TAR. Every stable should have a large pot of this delightfully smelling tar.

It is used externally as a preservative for the hoof and it is also perfect to pack in below leather soles of horses with brittle or dry hoofs.

When rubbed around the coronet it will stimulate the healthy growth of the wall and it can also be used as a mild blister. It is invaluable against thrush, sandcracks, seedy toes and the hoof in general.

It is a perfect antiseptic so always make sure you keep a pot handy – and know when to use it and when not!

STOCKING. White hair on the legs going past the fetlock.

STOCKMAN. The Australian version of the American cowboy.

STOCK WHIP. The stockman carries a long whip which he uses for cattle control.

STRANGLES. A contagious disease whose early signs are a yellow discharge, loss of appetite and a rise in temperature. Young animals are the ones most likely to succumb to the two forms of Strangles.

An abscess develops around the throat gland which eventually bursts; the discharging pus is highly infectious.

Horses can die from Strangles and, if they live, they can have their wind ruined so get the veterinarian without hesitation. Strict hygiene must be practised.

STRAW. See BEDDING.

STRINGHALT. The cause is unknown but the condition easy to see. The hind leg is lifted extra high, sometimes right up to the body. The shoes wear out quickly and the affected leg's foot makes a different sound when placed on the ground.

Stringhalt can appear at any age and gets progressively worse with little that anyone can do.

STUD. A place where horses are kept and bred. In America this word also means a stallion.

STUD GROOM. The man at the top of his trade who has spent his life with horses, who knows everything and who makes the best – though often toughest – teacher. The writer's knowledge all came from stud grooms of the old school. Now often called stable managers.

STUDS. These are screwed into the heels of the shoe in specially prepared holes. They are made from best steel and prevent slipping. They can also give a fallen rider terrible face injuries.

SUFFOLK PUNCH. A British breed of heavy draught horse named after the county of origin. Their colour is only ever chesnut – never chestnut. They can be as tall as a Clydesdale but are docile and very game with great strength, doing slow haulage work which would break the spirit of any other draught horse.

They have thick, powerful necks and no feather except for a tiny tuft at the fetlock.

SURCINGLE. See ROLLER. This means a roller in America. In Britain it means the under bellystrap on a rug.

SWAY BACKED. An animal whose back dips with age, weakness or bad conformation.

SWITCH TAIL. An undocked tail with the long hairs pulled neatly to a point.

TACK. The name used to describe the ridden horse's equipment apart from harness.

TAIL PULLING. This is a great art and makes the tail very neat. The hairs are pulled out from the top to a point half way down the bone.

TAKES HOLD. A hard mouthed or over keen animal who takes hold of his bit and goes without any 'by your leave' from the rider!

TAR. See STOCKHOLM TAR.

TEETH. See also under AGE. Horses do not suffer from tooth decay as much as us. They do not eat as much sugar rubbish! When tooth trouble does arise, though, get the professional in. You wouldn't like the do-it-yourself man attending to your teeth!

TEMPERAMENT. Nearly all living creatures have the ability to get angry and the horse is no exception although with this animal, it is usually the case that the anger follows fear.

In the past, though, there have been exceptions of horses that carried 'bad blood'. Decades ago, there was a famous jumping stallion called Cottage. He was vicious to the point of being evil and, sad to say, he passed on these genes to his offspring. Most animals who have Cottage in their name go back to him – and his temper. One Grand National winner who springs to mind is Sheila's Cottage. Her bad temper became the groom's nightmare.

It is said, truthfully that a breeder cannot hope to get a good tempered foal from a bad tempered dam, which makes sense. The foal copies what the mare does for the most formative portion of his life. If she kicks, bites and has a permanent hate-attitude to man, then obviously the foal will copy, thinking this is normal!

On the other hand, temper against man can arise from man's abuse so before you condemn an animal, try to check back where he has been, who has handled him and,

126

most important who broke him – and by what method.

It is possible, sometimes, to change a bad tempered horse's attitude but it requires considerable time and patience. And is this what you want to have to battle with when you buy a horse?

TEMPERATURE. The temperature of the normal adult horse before exercise is 100ºF, depending upon his age and the time of day. This is best taken per rectum.

TENDONS. These should be clean and free from swellings. They lie just behind the cannon bones. They can be sprained and ruptured.

TETANUS. Also commonly called Lockjaw, and a most serious condition requiring immediate Veterinary attention as well as medical attention for all humans.

It is caused by Clostridium Tetani in both animal and man and usually enters the body through a cut or other similar wound. Horses are very easily affected, possibly because of their close association with grass and soil, and most farming land, which receives manure, carries Tetanus in its earth.

Many owners inoculate their horses against this disease which makes toxins that are then absorbed into the general circulation of the body. It is extremely powerful. The early symptoms may be confusing and even misleading. The horse is stiff, not keen on moving about and, when he does work out, is very slow. He might carry his head higher than normal and it is stiff, almost rigid.

His breathing will become distressed and, on his face he will wear a look of enormous anxiety (see BODY LANGUAGE). After about one day and night the stiffness will increase, with the legs splayed out for balance. There will also be spasms which will start around the head and neck

127

then spread to the whole of the body.

Unless there is very swift action with more than a hefty dose of good luck, the horse can only deteriorate and die.

The same applies to man and tetanus has always been a battle-field affliction. It is vitally important that all people who associate with horses, or any animal of the soil, have themselves protected by their Doctor's recommended series of injections. These will be at a few weekly intervals, then a year, five years and finally ten years. A very efficient way to combat this most dreadful disease.

THIEF. A crafty horse as opposed to an honest one.

THORNS. Hunters often get thorns. Treat them as you would on yourself. Get them out with a clean needle but be gentle; then clean the puncture wound.

THOROUGHBRED. The world's fastest and most valuable horse. The British Thoroughbred has been exported the world over and he has also helped to found many half breeds.

He is really of foreign blood because he descended from certain Arabians imported into Britain. These were they Byerley Turk imported in 1689, the Alcock Arabian in 1700, the Darley Arabian in 1704 and the Godolphin Arabian in 1730. The Alcock Arabian is a grey, and all grey Thoroughbreds trace back to this magnificent animal.

The Darley Arabian was the sire of Flying Childers and the famous Eclipse is of this line. The Darley and Godolphin Arabians were bay; the Byerley Turk was black.

There were other imported horses who helped found the breed; the Leeds Arabian, the Lister Turk and the Darley White Turk. An Arabian mare called Old Bald Peg also exercised considerable influence on Thoroughbred breeding.

A Thoroughbred may be of nearly any colour though piebalds and skewbalds are virtually unknown. They are tall, fine strong looking animals and some still show their Arabian ancestry with the typical Arabian facial characteristics. They are highly strung and nervous. They do not take kindly to being bullied and some of them have doubtful tempers. They all require very experienced riders.

A Thoroughbred has tremendous courage and will die before quitting. No other horse can match him for sheer speed, and with the present-day arts of breeding, good stallions will fetch astronomical sums of money.

THOROUGH PIN. This is a soft swelling on either side of the hock or near the joint of the fetlock. It comes from strain and overwork. Get help.

THREE DAY EVENTS. One of the most famous is at Badminton, held on the estate of the Duke of Beaufort.

Three days are required for this test because it is an extensive one for both man and beast. It starts with a dressage test which is to find out whether the horse (and rider) has had the correct basic training. On the second day there comes the tough bit. There is a ride along a track or road which is roughly three miles long. This should be done at a brisk trot because this ride is timed. Directly afterwards comes the steeplechase course with about twelve fences which must be taken at the gallop. Then comes a second stretch with a short break for a breather for both. The vet checks the animals but ignores the humans: they don't really count, do they? This other bit is very arduous with tricky, large fences. There are often easy ways around that can be ridden but they take a longer time and time is of the essence. The third and final day is show jumping. The object here is to demonstrate how the horse has stood up to the foregoing.

Both rider and horse are pushed to the limit at a good Three Day Event like Badminton and the winner becomes a god. There are often many foreign riders entered for Badminton, especially when it is Olympic Year, as the result of this event usually predetermines the horses and riders selected by each country for the Olympic Games.

Good event horses are worth their weight in gold but the labour and hard work required to reach this high standard is only for the dedicated and affluent few, unless sponsorship can be obtained. The average person has no chance at all to enter something like Badminton because the general costs, insurances and other overheads are astronomical in price.

THRUSH. A nasty smelling condition of the foot caused by the horse standing for too long in filthy conditions. Put down really clean bedding and keep it clean! Cleanse the foot and apply Stockholm Tar in generous helpings to the cleft of the frog.

TOES. A horse on his toes is one who is so full of the joys of spring that he doesn't know which way to plunge next. Sit tight!

TOSS. When the rider leaves the saddle at the whim of the horse!

TOURNIQUET. This is applied in an emergency to stop bleeding. The blood is halted by pressure being applied on a limb pressure point with some hard object tightened by the aid of a stick put through a loop of string or other material. Do not leave in place for more than ten minutes at a time otherwise the limb can die from lack of blood.

TRACES. Parts of the harness running from the horse to the shafts, to connect it to a cart or carriage.

TRAINER. One who holds a licence to train race horses.

TRAINING TACKLE. The equipment used to break in a horse. This consists of the bridle and bit with keys, roller, crupper and long reins.

TREADS. Injuries to the horse's feet at the coronet when he treads on himself. These are usually only simple but require cleansing and dressing.

TROIKA. See NORTH FOREST.

TROT. The horse's second pace which can be ridden by posting up and down in the saddle or by sitting still. The horse's legs move diagonally

TROTTER. Horses who race at the trot pulling a small sulky. They wear special harness. Some of these animals pace as opposed to trot, i.e. their legs move together on the same side, first on the left and then on the right. This gives the horse a rolling gait but is very fast. Special harness is required.

TROTTING ON THE DIAGONALS. As we are right or left handed so is the horse. Some favour the right diagonal, others the left. It is easy to find out which. Study the horse at the trot. When the rider's seat is in the saddle see which shoulder is forward. That gives the diagonal. To change this the rider should miss a bump at the trot. He will immediately notice the difference in the gait as his seat comes down into the saddle with the other shoulder going forward.

Changing diagonals is good exercise for both rider and horse though some animals are crafty. They object to changing diagonals and will throw in an extra step and hey presto! – the rider finds himself back on the usual diagonal!

TUCKED UP. Describes animals in poor condition.

TURNED OUT. Describes horses turned out at grass after hard work.

TWITCH. A form of restraint approved by the RSPCA for fractious horses. A piece of rope is looped through a stick and twisted round the upper lip. The twitch becomes painful when the horse moves away, so it encourages him to stand still. Never put a twitch on an ear. That is cruelty.

There is a twitch called Galvayne's which goes over the poll.

UNDER STARTER'S ORDERS. Racers and jockeys under the starter's orders just before the race starts.

UNSEEN. The dodgy practice of buying a horse without looking at him!

UP FROM GRASS. A horse brought up from soft grass and living back in his stable to begin work and training again.

UP TO WEIGHT. A strong horse with strength and bone capable of carrying a heavy weight.

URINE. This is the liquid body waste which is expelled by the kidneys as being of no use to the body.

Humans urinate far more frequently than horses but they dung more than we do in the 24 hours. Diet answers this puzzle: we are omnivorous; they are herbivorous.

When a horse passes urine it is called staling and the amount passed depends entirely upon health, diet, work and age. Perhaps a reasonable average of urine for a horse of, say, 16 hands to pass in 24 hours is about 9 pints.

The horse's urine should not smell offensive. The colour should be a dim yellow and the urine should be expelled with force in a steady stream. Any urine which does not meet the above should make you think. If it has an acrid odour or is brown, perhaps starts as a stream then changes to a trickle, with the horse wearing a worried expression, that should be enough to concentrate your mind. Never delay calling your vet if you suspect urine trouble.

Urine for a herbivorous animal should be alkaline. A carnivorous animal's urine should be acid. We humans fall between the two scales.

The greatest danger is obstruction and retention of the urine. You must never hesitate to seek instant, professional help.

VENTILATION. Horses must have fresh air so do leave the top door open, but, if the wind is cruel, open the window instead!

VETERINARIAN. A highly qualified professional person who after years of training is registered and licensed to practise his calling. In other words, the animals' doctor.

VETERINARIAN'S CERTIFICATE. Popularly known as the Vet's Cert. When buying and selling, always be able to produce this so that it is known your animal has been passed sound in all aspects by a qualified practitioner. When selling, the seller pays for the certificate. If the buyer wants a horse that does not have a Vet's Cert. he must pay to have the horse examined and the Cert. issued. This is a bit like a surveyor's report on the house you would like to buy before you go in for the mortgage. A safeguard, a legal comeback.

VICE & VICIOUSNESS. These can be broken down to include bad habits, mild vices, erratic whims and positive hatred of man. In the latter case, the only usual answer is a bullet because the horse is a very powerful animal; man is puny alongside him and human life must always come first.

Crib biting and weaving (*q.v.*) often start out as mere bad habits from the horse's boredom. If he has been used to his freedom, then is locked in the stable for twenty-three hours a day, of course he is going to get bored and into mischief. So would you. Some horses decide that it is great fun to rip their clothing into sheds. Others prefer a methodical destruction of their stable. Kicking over the water bucket can be hilarious and leering at a human with ears back and rolling eyes makes his day. Another antic which can start as a game is to scratch his head with a hind leg. This, though, becomes hell when the hoof gets caught in the head collar. Panic floods the horse and the luckless human who has to release him runs considerable risk of physical injury.

Other vices are jibbing, bolting, backing wildly, bucking, and rearing, all of which may be extremely dangerous to the rider because control is lost. One of the most horrendous experiences the writer had was when, as a teenage groom, her horse reared suddenly. There was no warning, no reason, no time to react. The horse went up so high it lost its balance and came crashing backwards on the road. The writer only just managed to throw herself sideways and escape having her chest crushed. Even then, there were injuries because when a horse falls he panics. He does not give a damn for any other living creature. His atavistic instinct is to rise to his feet and bolt. This one did – after he had stamped all over the writer's legs – and he had just been shod. He was also a heavyweight brute! Any horse who rears just for the sheer hell of terrifying the rider is useless. Get rid of the brute; if necessary, with a bullet.

Bucking may or may not be a vice. If a horse has this down to a fine art and, when the rider is rolling in the grass, he then turns to kick him to bits, use said gun again. If however, he goes galloping off, it could well be he feels the sheer joy of life. In which case it is your fault for not taking the tickle from his toes first with plenty of long, hard, trotting!

Going into reverse swiftly is more than disconcerting to the rider. Remedial action must be taken with heels and stick forthwith and the same goes for jibbing. Act immediately.

Bolting is another matter. Why does the horse bolt? Is it his teeth? Does the bit hurt? You are supposed to have the brains, so investigate before you condemn the animal. Often the horse who bolts from the metal bit will respond in quite a civilised manner if ridden in a bitless bridle.

Rearing and striking with the forefeet is a dreadful vice. So much so that the writer says just put the animal down. Human life comes first; never forget that.

Kicking is another dangerous vice so think of the poor farrier who has to shoe such a brute. Again, this vice is very hard to check let alone cure; it is not worth bothering with such an animal. Put him down.

Biting is a wicked vice. A harsh slap across the face may steady the horse down but watch out when your back is turned. Usually this vice has come out because the young horse has received bad treatment from some fool of a groom. A muzzle can be used but this has to be removed for feeding which puts you back to square one again. Think hard whether such an animal is worth owning.

Shying can come from nervousness, downright fear of the unknown or the horse's general lack of confidence. This can be cured – usually – but it takes considerable time and patience on the part of the rider. He must build up a relationship of trust with his horse which can take many months. Whether the horse is worth this only the owner can decide.

Vice is such a highly complicated and important subject you are advised to study it in depth – for your own safety.

VOMITING. Everyone knows the warning symptoms of 'I'm going to be sick!' The mouth salivates furiously. There are often pains in the inside with a queasy headache and a general feeling of misery. Like ourselves, most mammals vomit through the mouth.

A horse does not. Luckily the horse does not vomit very often but, when he does, it is down his nostrils and it means something very serious indeed. Long before the animal has reached this stage, you will have alerted your vet.

The cause might be an obstruction in part of the gut, or a rupture of the stomach wall. Always remember that vomiting is an actual symptom; a warning that something has gone seriously wrong.

The writer had an experience of this when a teenage girl groom. A travelling stallion, who was in tip top health, quite suddenly after serving a mare began to show all the symptoms of internal distress. The vet was sent for but he was away on another urgent case. Gradually, this magnificent Thoroughbred showed increasing pain and distress then he began to vomit. It poured from his nostrils and, of course, he could not breath. Horses rarely understand that air can be taken in through the mouth like us or, say, dogs.

When the vet was able to arrive he took one look and put the animal down. A later post mortem showed that, in serving the mare, the animal had become so excited he had twisted then ruptured his guts. The stomach contents had flowed everywhere.

WALER. An old name for the Australian horses who were

136

shipped to India in the last century.

WALKOVER. If only one horse has been declared for a race, he is allowed to walk the course and claim first prize.

WALL EYES. Eyes which do not have any pigmentation.

WARBLES. Parasites which annoy horses during the summer. The warble fly lays her eggs under the animal's skin and this hatches into a small grub which grows there. Always check your horse's skin during the summer for small, suspicious lumps.

WAR HORSE. The great horse of Europe who had to be capable of carrying a knight with his armour, up to thirty and forty stones. They could rarely move above a slow trot.

WARRANTY. A guarantee, but one which can be hotly disputed in Court! Find out exactly what the warranty constitutes before buying. Don't try and argue it out after the sale!

WARTS. Like the human variety, small growths on the skin commonly found on the face. Consult the veterinarian.

WATER. Horses must always have plenty of fresh water and preferably running. Do not give too much on returning from long, hard and hot work.

WEAVING. This is a bad habit and may, by some, be classed as a vice. Certainly if the horse is to be sold it must be pointed out by the vendor if a court action is to be avoided!

It is a habit when horses swing their heads and necks from side to side so that the body weight goes from one hoof to the other. It usually arises from downright boredom, lack of exercise, nothing to do or look at.

This weaving habit affects the front muscles of the body and can, in time, make the horse stumble when it does go out. In a large yard, other horses may copy the habit so do not let it start.

Keep the animal exercised, and in the stable occupied with a finely packed hay net, and give him something to look at. Don't forget, he can't lean forward and switch the box on to pass the time of day like you.

Weaving can be prevented by tying the horse with double head ropes, one on each side. Another method is to affix to the stable door a large arched metal frame which just gives him enough room to extend his head but obstructs him from weaving.

A bad weaver is a horse with a vice which makes it difficult to sell with a warranty because weaving can make a horse nervous and, thus, dangerous to own.

WEED. A poor, miserable animal. One badly bred with the wrong conformation; unpleasing to the eye and lacking in character.

WEIGHED IN. Jockeys must weigh in and out with their saddles before and after races to check their weights are correct. See HANDICAP.

WELSH COB. A cob-type of the Welsh Pony breed that is short legged, of great strength and suitable to ride and drive.

WELSH PONY. A breed of pony from Wales where they run on the mountains. They should not exceed 12.2 hands for the ponies or 14.2 hands for cobs.

The pony's head is clean cut and alert with small ears and lively eyes. They have a wide colour range and are ideal for children as well as adults, being both tough and sure footed.

WET, COLD HORSE. When you return from riding or hunting and your horse is wet through and cold you see to him first. NOT yourself. It's you who have made him wet in the first place so dry him before yourself.

One of the best ways to start to do this is to put a thick layer of straw and I do mean thick, under the rug NOT the blanket. This starts the drying process off and lets the air in, at the same time.

Give the horse a bucket of tepid NOT cold water. The latter could give him colic if he is greedy. Give him a very good warm mash and mix in a little linseed oil if possible. Make sure his bed is thick. Encourage him to stale, i.e. pass urine, encouraging him if necessary with soft whistles.

Then strip off your coat, roll up your sleeves and start. You must get that coat dry before the horse catches a chill from too fast drying by rapid evaporation of moisture. Rubbing with towels, hay wisps, etc. all stimulates the blood and helps to promote dryness. Do dry his wet ears. If they stay wet, so will his body.

A bit of belly wet does not matter but it is vital the region over his kidneys is dried off thoroughly.

Some horses hate being mauled about like this when they are tired, so be understanding. Let him have his warm mash first and be well stuck into his hay net before you start your work. It takes time. It is hard but always remember, left to himself, no horse in his right mind would get himself covered with mud and sweat unnecessarily. Horses are not fools; they also like their creature comforts.

When the horse is dry, comfortable, warm, and wearing his stable blanket and rug then, and only then, are you allowed to go and attend to yourself. If you don't like this part of being with horses, then don't ride them or mix with them. Take up crochet work instead!

WHITE. A colour which needs no description but in the horse is always classed as grey – for some reason that has always baffled the writer!

WINALOT. This describes long, floppy ears. Often the sign of a lazy animal.

WINDGALLS. Puffy enlargements around the fetlock joints from concussion and too much road work. Rest the animal and treat with cold water and cold, wet bandages.

WIND SUCKING. See CRIB BITING and VICE.

WITHERS. The highest point of the horse in front of the saddle where his measurement is taken.

WORMS. All worms are parasites and these can never be taken lightly, whether the human or animal variety.

There are 11 Strongyles in horses, including ringworm (*q.v.*) and tapeworm, which cause anaemia, debility and often produce an intermittent cough. It is vital to call the vet and sensible to worm the animal on a regular basis to the vet's instructions.

Never forget that some worm eggs can be transmitted to humans!

WOUNDS. Treat as for yourself. If serious get professional help. If minor, cleanse and dress.

XANTHOS. An ancient Greek name for the Palomino colouring.

YARD. The name for a group of stables, which are often in a square. A good yard has the stables facing the sun with the tack and forage rooms facing the shade. There may be clean gravel and a centre piece of well cut grass. The whole, a joy to behold.

YEARLING. A horse of one year. With Thoroughbreds their official age is counted from New Year's Day, irrespective of their real age, so for one of this breed born on December 31st, when one day old on January 1st officially he will be aged one year.

YEW. All yew trees are poisonous to the horse. The only quick remedy is a rapid drench. A good stimulant in coffee or raw linseed oil. Don't put your horse near a yew tree! See POISONOUS PLANTS.

YORKSHIRE COACH HORSE. A Yorkshire animal bred solely for carriage work and still used on stately occasions. The breed is an offshoot of the Cleveland Bay though Yorkshire horses are taller and have more style. The colours are bay and brown with black points.

YOUNGSTER. A horse under four years of age.

ZOONOSES. The official name for an animal disease which can be caught by man and the best word the writer could find to end this A to Z book!

In a vet's dictionary there are so many diseases transmutable between man and beast that it is enough to make the straightest hair curl wildly. Just a few are worms like ringworm and tapeworm. There is Equine Infectious Anaemia, Glanders (*q.v.*) and, though rare in this country, Equine *Encephalomyelitis*. This latter produces a paralysis of the head and neck muscles. It features in North and South America, Mexico, Russia and the Far and Middle East.

In 1971 thousands of horses died from this latter disease in the USA and Mexico, which led to Britain imposing severe import restrictions on horses coming from that region to Britain. Again it was prevalent in 1975 in the USA.

However there is now a vaccine available.

Useful Addresses:

THE BRITISH HORSE SOCIETY, Stoneleigh Deer Park, Stareton, Kenilworth, Warwicks, CV8 2XZ. Tel. 01203 707700

THE ASSOCIATION OF BRITISH RIDING SCHOOLS, Queen's Chambers, 38-40 Queen Street, Penzance, Cornwall, TR18 4BH. Tel. 01736 369440